# Daily MATH JUMPSTARTS

## LAURIE STEDING

New York · Toronto · London · Auckland · Sydney
Mexico City · New Delhi · Hong Kong · Buenos Aires

**Teaching** *Resources*

KORE DAY

Content editing by Merideth Anderson
Copy editing by Sarah Glasscock
Cover design by Maria Lilja
Interior design by Kelli Thompson
ISBN-13: 978-0-545-11003-7
ISBN-10: 0-545-11003-3

# Contents

# Introduction

**W**hat tremendous strides math education has made in the past ten years! There is so much information to share with children, and so little time to fit more into our already over-scheduled days. That's why this book was written—to help you target the key areas covered by your curriculum and connected to the NCTM standards, through focused problem-solving time each day. The problems in this book are designed to stimulate students' curiosity about everyday math concepts, such as how to divide a pizza fairly among a group of friends, and to give them immediate feedback as you check the problem on the board or on-screen.

## About the Problems

*Daily Math Jumpstarts* provides a year's worth of daily math problems, set on reproducible pages, which can be photocopied and displayed on a projection screen. In this way, students can work independently to solve the problems and then share solutions in a whole-class setting.

All the problems in this book have been grouped into key curriculum areas and aligned to the new NCTM Standards and are designed to supplement a well-rounded math curriculum. The problems appear three to a page, so while you may decide to focus on one problem each day, you also may want to photocopy two pages at the beginning of the week so that students can work at their own pace.

**This flexible format allows you to**

- **photocopy a single practice page for class work or homework**

- **focus on one or two problems in a daily review at the overhead or on the interactive whiteboard**

- **photocopy the pages on stock paper, cut apart the problems, and organize them in a problem-solving file at a math center.**

**Note:** A few problems in each chapter require students to use a reproducible chart or activity page. These pages are included at the end of each chapter and are easily reproduced. You'll see problems marked with the symbol shown here.

Each chapter also includes a "Curriculum Connections" section (see below) which describes more-in-depth activities designed to give students extra practice with skills and concepts that often need more attention.

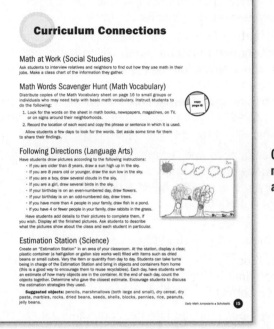

**Curriculum Connections pages help you extend math concepts students have been practicing and apply them in other subject areas.**

## Making the Most of the *Daily Math Jumpstart* Problems

Because students come to us with a variety of skills, they will find that some problems may seem difficult, while others may seem easy. Preview the problems and activities you assign to give students opportunities to demonstrate their strengths as well as opportunities to explore and practice skills that need strengthening. (To differentiate, you might assign similar problems at different levels, give additional information or strategies to scaffold a specific problem, or provide the solution to an example that is similar in format to the one you want students to solve independently.)

Although the problems and activities in this book take only a short period of time to do, it is important to spend a few minutes reviewing and discussing the reasoning and strategies students used to arrive at their answers. Providing an environment in which children discuss, demonstrate, and justify their mathematical thinking will encourage them to take some intellectual risks and expose them to new ways of doing math.

Finally, please use these problems and activities flexibly; you may assign them in any order that meets your curricular needs and you may give them to students at any time that works best for your schedule: at the beginning or end of each day, during transition times, or to provide a lively introduction to the math period. You might want to assign the problems for homework as well, and then discuss the answers in class.

**Enjoy** using this book to stretch your students' minds a bit each day, and to help them see that math is fun!

# NCTM Standards

The National Council of Teachers of Mathematics published 10 standards that the council considers essential to any elementary math curriculum. Each problem in *Daily Math Jumpstarts* lists the standards it supports by number. The following briefly summarizes each standard:

❶ **NUMBER AND OPERATIONS:** Understand whole numbers, fractions, and decimals; develop the ability to estimate, relate operations to one another, and compute numbers fluently. These are the basic building blocks of mathematics.

❷ **ALGEBRA:** Understand patterns, relations, and functions in real-world situations; represent and analyze mathematical situations and structures using algebraic symbols; analyze change in various contexts. Gaining proficiency in these skills helps students develop a sense of mathematically based relationships in the world around them.

❸ **GEOMETRY AND SPATIAL SENSE:** Recognize 2- and 3-dimensional shapes, their properties, and the relationships among shapes; know the effects of changes on shapes. Gaining proficiency in these skills helps students understand and describe the physical world around them.

❹ **MEASUREMENT:** Learn and practice measuring to strengthen and formalize intuitive comparisons of length, width, height, capacity, weight, mass, area, volume, time, temperature, and angle. Gaining proficiency in these skills also helps students understand and describe the physical world around them.

❺ **DATA ANALYSIS AND PROBABILITY:** Collect, organize, describe, display, and interpret data; explore concepts of chance. Gaining proficiency in these skills gives students opportunities to investigate and analyze the world around them.

❻ **PROBLEM SOLVING:** Apply mathematical skills confidently and meaningfully to unfamiliar situations. This is the overarching goal of math instruction.

❼ **REASONING:** Analyze, draw conclusions, and justify one's thinking. Gaining proficiency in these skills helps students develop a sense of self-reliance and confidence in their mathematical abilities and helps them see how thinking mathematically makes sense.

❽ **COMMUNICATION:** Use tools, such as reading, writing, modeling, drawing, and discussing, to explore, convey, and clarify mathematical concepts and ideas.

❾ **MATHEMATICAL CONNECTIONS:** Notice how concepts and ideas in one area of math relate to other areas of math, other subject areas, and one's everyday life. Gaining awareness of mathematical connections fosters an appreciation of the usefulness of mathematics.

❿ **REPRESENTATION:** Create and use representations to organize, record, and communicate mathematical ideas. Students must acquire the ability to select, apply, and translate among mathematical representations to solve many different types of math problems.

# Chapter 1
# Everyday Math

## 1. Math for Dinner

List at least four different ways you can use math when eating pizza with your friends.

1.

2.

3.

4.

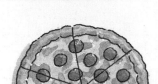

## 2. Math in Sports

List at least three ways you can use math words when you're playing sports. Identify the sport or sports with each math word.

*Example:* swimming: measure the time it takes to swim 100 meters

1.

2.

3.

## 3. Math in Weather Forecasts

What math words do you use when you talk about the weather? List at least four words.

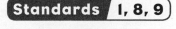

1.

2.

3.

4.

## 4. Comparing and Ordering Sports Scores

Standards  1, 9

Write down four different sports and make up final game scores for each. Now write the sports in order from greatest number of points to least number of points.

| Sport | Final Game Score | Order: greatest to least (1–4) |
|---|---|---|
|  |  |  |
|  |  |  |
|  |  |  |
|  |  |  |

## 5. Making Math Sense

Standards  1, 6, 8, 9

Fredric likes to exaggerate when he talks. Rewrite each exaggeration of Fredric's below so that it is believable.

a. I was on an airplane that flew across the country in 15 minutes!

_____

b. I only need 30 seconds of sleep every night!

_____

c. Last night it rained 2 feet in my backyard!

_____

## 6. Making More Math Sense

Standards  1, 8, 9

A news announcer on the radio made this report: "A bank robber got away from the First National Bank with 5,000 cents. He escaped in a car that sped away at 70 feet per hour. Police set up a roadblock on Main Street and captured the crook. Now, we'll pause for a commercial break. We'll continue this story in 1 year." Below, write the three words that don't make sense and write a better substitute for each.

**Words From Problem**          **Substitute Words That Make Sense**

_____          _____

_____          _____

_____          _____

## 7. Comparing Ways to Travel

Standards | 1, 6, 8

Six friends are having a race to find out who can travel around the block the fastest. They each travel a different way: Sally saunters, Tania trots, Marcus marches, Toshio tiptoes, Sarah strides, and Jaime jogs. Write their names in the order you think they will finish the race.

1. _____    4. _____

2. _____    5. _____

3. _____    6. _____

## 8. Making a Schedule

Standards | 1, 4, 6, 9

Your neighbor Jasmine is always late for school. Her mom asks you to help her get there on time. List the things Jasmine probably needs to do in the morning before school. Beside each item on your list, write the amount of time you think it should take her to do it. For example:

| Activity | Time |
|---|---|
| Get dressed | 5 minutes |
|  |  |
|  |  |
|  |  |

How much time will it take Jasmine to do all the things on the list?

_____

If she needs to leave for school at 8:00, what is the latest time she can get up?

_____

## 9. Completing a Word Problem

Standards | 1, 6, 8

Write a question to complete the following word problem:

Amber and her sister went to the store to buy hats. Amber bought a hat that cost $4.50. Amber's sister bought a hat on sale for $3.95.

_____

_____ ?

Write the entire problem on the back of this page, and write the solution on a separate piece of paper. Trade problems with a classmate and solve. Check each other's work.

## 10. Calculating Costs

"The wind knocked down part of my fence," groaned Ms. Diaz, "and it's going to cost a lot of money to fix it."

What does Ms. Diaz need to know before she can figure out how much it will cost to repair the fence?

- _____
- _____
- _____
- _____

---

## 11. Measuring Time

List these situations in order from the shortest (1) to the longest (5) amount of time you would spend waiting:

_____ waiting to get a drink of water from the fountain

_____ waiting for food in a restaurant

_____ waiting for a birthday or special holiday

_____ waiting for a bus

_____ waiting your turn in a game

Which situations might take about the same amount of time? _____ and

_____

---

## 12. Numerical Prefixes

Tell how these words are related. *Hint: What do they have in common?*

triple play    tripod    triplets    tricycle    trio    triathlon

What are some words that mean "two of something"?

_____

_____

_____

Draw a picture for one of these words.

## 13. Comparing Sale Prices

Standards | 1, 6

Ana went to the mall to shop for jeans. She found a pair that was on sale for ⅓ off the regular price, and another pair that was on sale for ¼ off the regular price. Write the steps Ana needs to follow to find which pair of jeans has the lower price.

**Steps:**

1. _____

2. _____

3. _____

4. _____

---

## 14. Using Coupons to Save

Standards | 1, 6, 9

Willy's mom said that if he clips coupons for things she needs to buy and helps her shop, he can keep the money saved by using the coupons. List five things that they might buy using coupons.

1. _____     4. _____

2. _____     5. _____

3. _____

How can Willy keep track of how much money they saved?

_____

---

## 15. Using Relationships Between Prices

Standards | 1, 7, 8, 9

Create prices for the following items so that a pair of jeans costs half as much as a pair of sneakers but twice as much as a T-shirt.

Pair of jeans $_____

Pair of sneakers $_____

T-shirt $_____

> **Now, write a math problem like this one. Solve it with a partner.**

## 16. Days, Months, and Seasons

Standards 1, 4, 6, 9

Drifting on a raft in the middle of the ocean, a man spent over 120 days alone before being rescued!

About how many months is 120 days? _____

What season was it 120 days ago? _____

List four things that you have done or that have happened to you during the last 120 days.

1.

2.

3.

4.

## 17. Things That Come in a Dozen

Standards 1, 8, 9, 10

Name and draw at least three things that are grouped or packaged in sets of 12.

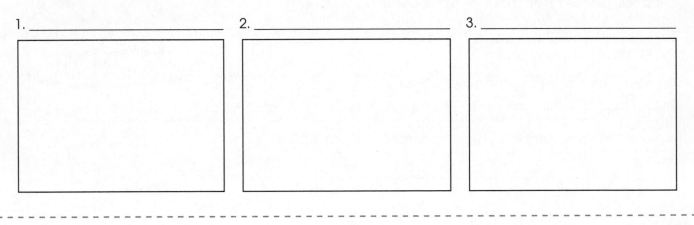

1. _____   2. _____   3. _____

## 18. Your Special Product

Standards 1, 6, 8, 9, 10

Imagine that you could make something to sell in a set, such as a set of cards or game pieces. What would you create and how many would you sell in a set? Write or draw your idea below.

On the back of this page, write a word problem that uses your set. Give it to a partner to solve.

## 19. Venn Diagrams

Standards 5, 8, 10

Label one of the Venn diagram circles *Me* and the other circle with the name of a member of your family. In the circle labeled *Me*, list characteristics that describe you, but not your family member. In the other circle, list characteristics that describe your family member, but not you. In the space where the circles intersect, list characteristics you both share. (Try to compare characteristics with numbers and amounts, such as height and number of TV shows you watch per night.)

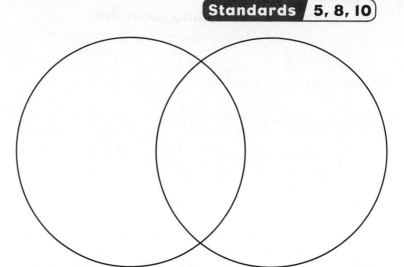

## 20. Venn Diagrams

Standards 3, 5, 9, 10

Copy the Venn diagram shown here on a separate piece of paper. Make it large to fill the page. Label the circles *Bumpy*, *Round*, and *Small*. Write the following words in the circle or intersection where they belong. (Some objects may not belong in any circle.)

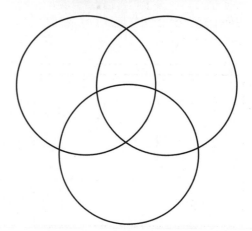

| | | |
|---|---|---|
| orange | marble | bulletin board |
| clock | apple | dictionary |
| cookie | tree | thumb tack |
| dice | roll of paper towels | |

## 21. Personalized Venn Diagrams

Standards 3, 5, 8, 9, 10

Draw a two or three-circle Venn diagram. Decide on the categories, such as *Dogs* and *Cats,* and label the circles. Write characteristics in the circles, such as *meows* for cats and *barks* for dogs. In the area where the circles intersect, write shared characteristics, such as *four-legged*.

## 22. Logical Thinking

Standards 6, 7, 9

Everyone in the Janek family has an opinion about what to have for dessert. The choices are ice cream, chocolate cake, apple pie, and oatmeal cookies. Read what each family member says, and choose the dessert they all can agree on eating.

Cal says, "I don't want to eat anything cold."
Ella says, "I've eaten all the fruit I need for today."
Derek says, "I shouldn't eat chocolate."
Freda says, "I'm allergic to apples."

**Best choice:**

ice cream     chocolate cake     apple pie     oatmeal cookies

---

## 23. Finding Needed Information

Standards 1, 5, 9

What information would you need to know in order to make a good estimate of the number of school lunches the students in your school today will eat today?

**Information:**

- _____

- _____

- _____

- _____

---

## 24. Making and Adjusting Estimates

Standards 1, 9

Choose a book without many pictures on its pages. Open it and look at one of the pages.

a. Write an estimate of how many words you think are on the page. First estimate: _____

b. Count the number of words in the first line of the page, and the number of lines on the page.

   Estimate the total number of words again, using this information. Second estimate: _____

c. Is the second estimate different from your first estimate? _____

d. Now count the words to find the actual word count.

Actual word count: _____

Which estimate was closer to the actual word count? _____

# Curriculum Connections

## Math at Work (Social Studies)

Ask students to interview relatives and neighbors to find out how they use math in their jobs. Make a class chart of the information they gather.

## Math Words Scavenger Hunt (Math Vocabulary)

Distribute copies of the Math Vocabulary sheet on page 16 to small groups or individuals who may need help with basic math vocabulary. Instruct students to do the following:

1. Look for the words on the sheet in math books, newspapers, magazines, on TV, or on signs around their neighborhoods.

2. Record the location of each word and copy the phrase or sentence in which it is used.

   Allow students a few days to look for the words. Set aside some time for them to share their findings.

## Following Directions (Language Arts)

Have students draw pictures according to the following instructions:

- If you are older than 8 years, draw a sun high up in the sky.
- If you are 8 years old or younger, draw the sun low in the sky.
- If you are a boy, draw several birds in the sky.
- If you are a girl, draw several clouds in the sky.
- If your birthday is on an even-numbered day, draw flowers.
- If your birthday is on an odd-numbered day, draw trees.
- If you have more than 4 people in your family, draw fish in a pond.
- If you have 4 or fewer people in your family, draw rabbits in the grass.

Have students add details to their pictures to complete them, if you wish. Display all the finished pictures. Ask students to describe what the pictures show about the class and each student in particular.

## Estimation Station (Science)

Create an "Estimation Station" in an area of your classroom. At the station, display a clear, plastic container (a half-gallon or gallon size works well) filled with items such as dried beans or small cubes. Vary the item or quantity from day to day. Students can take turns being in charge of the Estimation Station and bring in objects and containers from home (this is a good way to encourage them to reuse recyclables). Each day, have students write an estimate of how many objects are in the container. At the end of each day, count the objects together. Determine who gave the closest estimate. Encourage students to discuss the estimation strategies they used.

**Suggested objects:** pencils, marshmallows (both large and small), dry cereal, dry pasta, marbles, rocks, dried beans, seeds, shells, blocks, pennies, rice, peanuts, jelly beans.

# Math Vocabulary Words

| equivalent | fewer | greater | sum | difference |
| --- | --- | --- | --- | --- |
| more | less | total | product | percent |
| under | over | between | equal | value |
| capacity | increase | average | range | about |

# Chapter 2
# Addition and Subtraction

## 1. A Fairy Tale Addition Problem

If the bears (but not Goldilocks) invited the pigs (but not the wolf) and the billy goats (but not the troll) over for a party, how many animals would be at the party? Draw a picture to show your answer.

On the back of this page, write a problem of your own that uses numbers from stories.

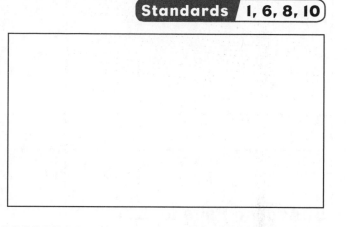

## 2. Adding Points

Suppose colors were assigned the following points:

purple = 6 points          red = 5 points          green = 4 points          yellow = 3 points
blue = 2 points            white = 1 point         (Other colors = 0 points)

Look at your clothing. Count each color only once in each piece of clothing.

What is your color point total? _____

Make up your own color point system.

purple = _____ points     red = _____ points     green = _____ points     yellow = _____ points

blue = _____ points      white = _____ point     (Other colors = _____ points)

Add up your points again. How does your new total compare with your first total? _____

_____

## 3. Adding Points

Suppose each letter of the alphabet is worth points. The letter A is worth 1 point,
B is worth 2 points, C is worth 3 points, and so on, up to Z, which is worth 26 points.
On another piece of paper, make a table to show how many points each letter is worth.

Using this point system, add up the letters that make up each part of your name. For example the name ANN would be 1(A) + 14(N) + 14(N) = 29 points.

First name: _____     _____ points

Middle name: _____     _____ points

Last name: _____     _____ points

Which part of your name is worth the most points?

_____

## 4. Illustrating and Writing a Word Problem

Standards  1, 6, 8, 10

Think of an addition problem that has 14 as its sum. First draw a picture of the problem. Next write it as a word problem.

Word problem:

Picture

---

## 5. Addend Pairs for 100

Standards 1, 7

On a separate piece of paper, write all the different combinations of two whole numbers that add up to 100. Write each fact only once. Since the order of addends does not change the sum, do not repeat combinations. (For example, 51 + 49 is the same as 49+ 51. List only one.)

How many combinations did you find? _____

What strategies did you use to find them?

_____

_____

---

## 6. Writing Addition Sentences for the Number 50

Standards 1, 8

On a separate piece of paper, write 10 addition sentences for the number 50. You can have as many addends in each addition sentence as you'd like. For example, 10 + 10 + 10 + 20 = 50.

How many different addition number sentences did you make? _____

Do you think there are still more addition sentences you could write for the number 50? Explain.

_____

_____

_____

## 7. Writing Addend Pairs

Standards 1, 2

Complete the Number Buddies chart (page 26). Write two numbers on each T-shirt that, when added together, equal the number of the row. For example, in row 6 you can complete the number buddies to show 6 + 0, 0 + 6, 5 + 1, 1 + 5, and so on.

copy
page 25

$6+0$

$0+6$

---

## 8. Addition Rules

Standards 1, 2, 7

Complete each sentence below to write four addition rules. Then prove each rule is true by showing a number sentence that satisfies the rule.

1. The sum of an odd number and an odd number is always _____.

   Proof: _____

2. The sum of an even number and an even number is always _____.

   Proof: _____

3. The sum of an odd number and an even number is always _____.

   Proof: _____

4. If you change the order of the addends, the sum _____.

   Proof: _____

---

## 9. Writing Numbers

Standards 1, 7

Use the digits 2, 4, 5, and 8 to write two 2-digit numbers whose sum is 100. Write two possible answers.

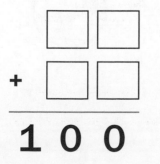

## 10. Using Mental Math

Use mental math to find the answer to each question.
Tell what strategy you used for each one.

a. What number comes after 17 + 8? _____

   Strategy: _____

b. Which is greater, 21 + 11 or 20 + 14? _____

   Strategy: _____

c. What is 68 + 42? _____

   Strategy: _____

## 11. Determining Points for a Score

Look at the Addition Target (page 26). In 3 rounds,
throwing once each round, Harry got 37 points and Kim
got 42 points. Write a number sentence to show the
number of points Harry and Kim scored on each turn
to get their totals.

copy
page 26

   Kim: _____ + _____ + _____ = 42

   Harry: _____ + _____ + _____ = 37

## 12. Right on Target

Use the Addition Target (page 26) and 4 small, light
objects, such as paper clips. Place the target flat on
a desk. Close your eyes and drop the objects onto
the target area. Add the points of the sections on
which they land. Play 3 rounds, and record your totals
for each round below.

copy
page 26

Round 1 _____

Round 2 _____

Round 3 _____

## 13. Subtracting Money

Standards I, 6, 8

Mrs. Hernandez told her daughter that each time she didn't have her daily chore done by supper time, $0.10 would be subtracted from her allowance of $2.25 a week. At the end of the week, her daughter received $1.85 for her allowance. How many times was she late doing her chore?

_____

 Show your work:

## 14. Subtracting Cookies

Standards I, 6, 8

Linda's aunt made 2 dozen cookies. She told Linda and her cousins not to eat more than half the cookies. Linda ate 4 cookies, Michael ate 3 cookies, Caroline ate 6 cookies, and Kelsey ate 2 cookies. Did they eat more than half the cookies? Explain.

_____

_____

_____

_____

## 15. Comparing Expressions

Standards I, 7

Without subtracting, compare these two expressions:

335 – 49          497 – 72

Explain which expression has the greater number for an answer.

_____

_____

_____

_____

## 16. Extra, Extra! Subtraction's All Around You!

Standards 1, 8, 9

Write a news article about your class. The article must include at least one subtraction situation. For example, you might write: *On Thursday, 17 of Mrs. Chung's 30 fourth graders brought their lunch to school. The other 13 students ate the school lunch of macaroni and cheese...*

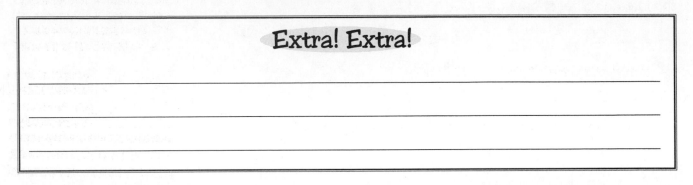

### Extra! Extra!

---

## 17. I Spy Marbles!

Standards 1, 6, 8, 10

Julie bought a bag of 28 marbles at the store. When she got home, she discovered there was a hole in the bag, and only 9 marbles were left! How many marbles did Julie lose between the store and home? Draw a picture that shows the problem.

---

## 18. Drawing a Picture to Solve a Problem

Standards 1, 2, 6, 8, 10

The Cardinals Mighty Sluggers baseball team has 11 players. The team's uniforms are red. At one game, 7 players wore red socks. Three of the players with red socks were also wearing red sweatshirts. Draw a picture to answer the following questions and write a subtraction sentence for each answer.

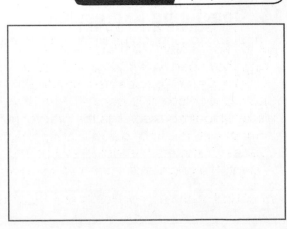

a. How many were not wearing red socks or sweatshirts?

_____

b. How many were not wearing red socks?

_____

c. How many were not wearing red sweatshirts?

_____

## 19. Differences in Flags

**Standards** | 1, 9, 10

On today's United States flag, each star represents a state. On the American flag of 1776, each star represented one of the United Colonies. Use the pictures of the flags to answer these questions:

a. How many states are there in the United States today?

_____

b. How many colonies were there in 1776?

_____

c. How many more states than colonies do the flags show?

_____

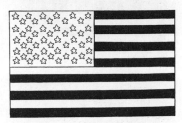

## 20. Adding and Subtracting Money

**Standards** | 1, 7

Grapes and strawberries cost $1.00 total. The grapes cost 10¢ less than the strawberries. Use mental math to find the price of each snack.

Grapes: _____          Strawberries: _____

 Now check it. Show your work:

## 21. Using Information in a Table to Solve a Problem

**Standards** | 1, 6, 7, 10

Ms. Kember's class is baking cookies as a special treat. They need to decide what kind of cookies to make. Of the 26 students in the class, 3 students dislike chocolate chip cookies and 12 students dislike ginger cookies. Eighteen students like cookies with raisins and 20 students like sugar cookies. Complete the table to show how many students like and dislike each kind of cookie.

What kind or kinds of cookies should the class make?

_____

_____

| Cookie Type | # Who Like It | # Who Don't Like It |
|---|---|---|
|  |  |  |
|  |  |  |
|  |  |  |
|  |  |  |

# Curriculum Connections

**Price List**

Wheels .... $0.40

Long boards $1.40

Short boards $0.75

Dials $0.65

Wires  $0.50

Tubes $0.35

Lights $0.80

## Marvelous Machines (Science)

Explain to students that they are going to invent machines! Have them work in small groups to brainstorm and decide what task their machine will perform. Then tell groups to draw the machine, making sure to include parts from the list below, and calculate the total cost of their machines. Each group can present its drawing to the class, explaining what the machine does and the cost. The class can create award categories such as most interesting machine, least expensive machine, machine with the most parts, and so on. They can then vote or identify which group receives each award.

## Exercise Equations (Sports and Recreation)

Make a class list of the 10 most popular exercise movements, such as touching toes or twisting at the waist. Specify a number of repetitions and assign points to each exercise. For example, deep knee bends (5 times)—10 points. Post the list so everyone can see it.

Have students working in small groups create short (3–5 minute) exercise routines consisting of exercises listed in the chart. Each group can teach the rest of the class its routine, and students can write number sentences to find how many points the routine is worth. Ask questions such as, "How could you change the routine so the total number of points is 10 points less? Ten points greater?"

## Addition Stones (Sports and Recreation)

This is a Native American game. For playing pieces you will need four smooth stones. Draw a different one of the simple designs shown below on one side of each stone. The other side of each stone remains blank.

Players take turns placing the stones in a container, shaking the container, and spilling the stones onto a hard surface. They receive points for each design showing, according to the chart below. They add the points for their total score. The player with the greatest score after three rounds wins.

Blank side of stones = 0 points          Moon = 5 points          Star = 10 points

Sun = 15 points          Snowflake = 20 points

moon          star          sun          snowflake

# Number Buddies

# Addition Target

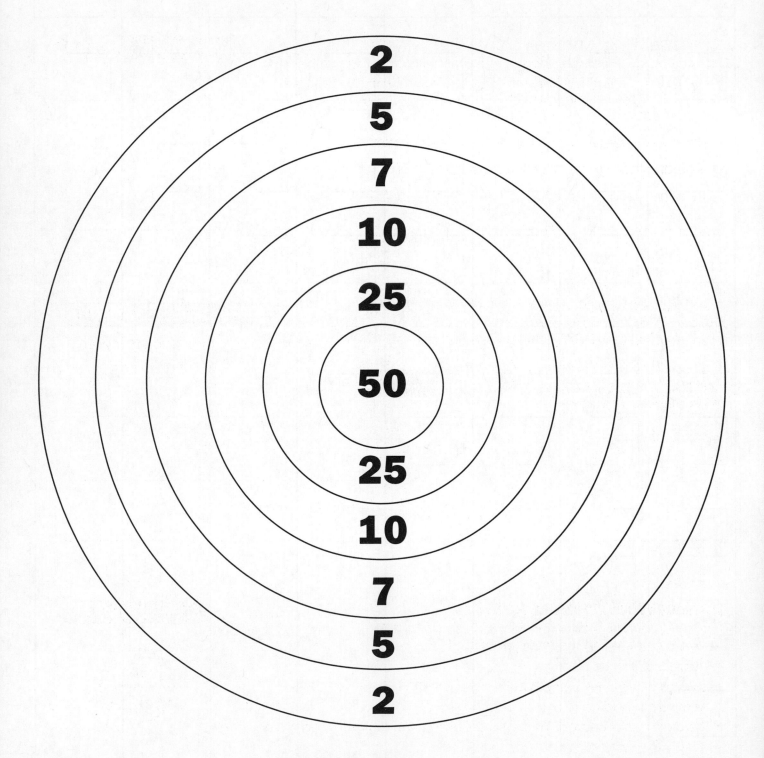

# Chapter 3
# Number Lines and Place Value

## 1. Visualizing Number Lines

Standards | 1, 3, 10

Picture or draw a number line starting with 0 with only odd numbers marked. The number line would start 0, 1, 3, 5, 7, 9, and 11. Continue along the number line in this manner until you reach the next odd number that:

a. has the same digit in both the tens and the ones places. _____

b. is greater than 40, and has a number in the tens place that is 5 less

  than the number in the ones place. _____

$\longleftarrow$——————————————————————————————$\longrightarrow$
0

## 2. What Number Am I?

Standards | 1, 7, 10

Visualize or draw a number line from 10 to 25 and then use these clues to find the mystery number:

• I'm between 15 and 20.
• I'm an odd number.
• I'm closer to 15 than to 20.

What number am I? _____

Write clues of your own for a different mystery number. The number must be described in exactly three clues

• _____

• _____

• _____

What number am I? _____

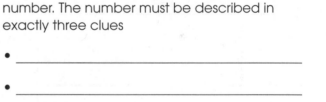

## 3. *Now* What Number Am I?

Standards | 1, 3

Use the Numeral Cards, the Place-Value Chart, and the following clues to find the mystery number:

• I have 3 digits.
• My digit in the ones place is 2 less than the digit in my tens place.
• All my digits add up to 5.
• The digit in my hundreds place is the same as the digit in my ones place.

What number am I? _____

copy
pages
32, 33

## 4. Give Me Your Digits

Use the Numeral Cards to show your 7-digit phone number.
Place this set of cards on the Place Value Chart.

- Write your telephone number in words.
- Write your telephone number in expanded form.
- Rearrange the digits of your phone number to make the greatest number possible using all 7 digits.
- Rearrange the digits of your phone number to make the least number possible using all 7 digits.

✏️ Show your work:

---

## 5. Writing Greatest and Least Numbers

Choose three cards from the Numeral Cards page. Complete the table below by writing the greatest number that can be formed using the three digits and the least number that can be formed using the three digits. Repeat, drawing three cards at a time until you have written five pairs.

| Greatest | Least |
|----------|-------|
|          |       |
|          |       |
|          |       |
|          |       |
|          |       |

Now, using the 10 numbers from the table above, order them from least to greatest.

_____, _____, _____, _____, _____, _____, _____, _____, _____, _____

---

## 6. Adding Using a Place-Value Chart

Use the Numeral Cards to find the sum of each problem below by placing the addends on the Place-Value Chart.

a.    $2 + 4 =$ _____

b.   $12 + 4 =$ _____

c.   $32 + 4 =$ _____

d.  $102 + 4 =$ _____

e. $2,582 + 4 =$ _____

What pattern do you notice? _____

## 7. Adding and Subtracting on a Number Line

Standards 1, 3, 8, 10

Visualize or draw a number line. Identify the number that you land on if you follow the directions below:

a. Start at 2.
b. Move ahead 5.
c. Go back 3.
d. Move ahead 4.

The number is: _____

Write a number sentence to describe how you moved along the number line. _____

## 8. Estimating Number of Breaths Taken

Standards 1, 8, 9

If you take 20 breaths per minute, calculate how many breaths you take in:

1 hour _____

1 day _____

1 week _____

1 year _____

✏️ Show your work:

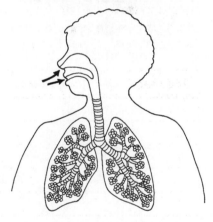

## 9. Money Equivalencies

Standards 1, 6, 8

Students at the Escalante Elementary School decided to save pennies to buy something special for the school. They saved 10,000 pennies! How many dollars did they save? Explain your answer in writing or with an illustration on the back of this page.

## 10. How Much Money Do You Make Each Day?

Standards 1, 9

Suppose a basketball player just signed a contract for $100 million dollars, to be paid over the next 5 years.

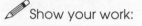
Show your work:

a. What will his salary be each year? _____

b. About how much money is that each month? _____

c. About how much money is that each day? _____

## 11. Numbers of Years

Standards 1, 6, 8

Todd's great-grandmother turns 100 years old today. About how many days has she lived? _____ How many decades are there in 100 years? _____ What word means "100 years"? _____

Show your work:

## 12. Out-of-This-World Distances

Standards 1, 4, 6, 9

Of all the large planetary bodies in our solar system, Mercury is the closest to the sun. It is 58,000,000 kilometers away from the sun. Pluto, a dwarf planet, is located 5,900,000,000 kilometers away from the sun. How far apart are Mercury and Pluto?

_____

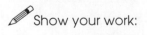
Show your work:

# Curriculum Connections

## On the Number Line (Physical Education)

This game can be played with a large or small group of students. One player is the caller. The other players pretend they are standing on number lines (so they need to leave plenty of space on either side of them). Have them put a marker on 0 for reference. The caller identifies the number players are to start on. Then the caller calls out another number, and the players move the number of steps to the left or right necessary to put them on the new number. The caller continues, calling out other numbers for players to move to along their number lines. Players take turns being the caller.

You may also have the caller call out the number of steps to take, and in which direction, and have players tell what number they move to.

## Math Superlatives (Language Arts)

Have students bring in ads and clippings from newspapers and magazines which include words such as *the most, the biggest, the longest*, and so on. Ask them to identify what is being measured and what the measurement is. Discuss whether they think the claim is accurate.

## Big Events  (Language Arts)

Gather newspaper and magazine articles that use numbers in the thousands, millions, billions, and beyond. Have students copy the numbers onto index cards. They can put the cards in order from least to greatest, practice reading the numbers, and match them with their corresponding articles.

## Map Skills (Social Studies)

The Great Wall of China is more than 2,000 miles long. Have students look on a map of the United States, and use the scale to find pairs of cities about 2,000 miles apart.

# Numeral Cards

| | | | | |
|---|---|---|---|---|
| 0 | 0 | 0 | 1 | 1 |
| 1 | 2 | 2 | 2 | 3 |
| 3 | 3 | 4 | 4 | 4 |
| 5 | 5 | 5 | 6 | 6 |
| 6 | 7 | 7 | 7 | 8 |
| 8 | 8 | 9 | 9 | 9 |

# Place-Value Chart

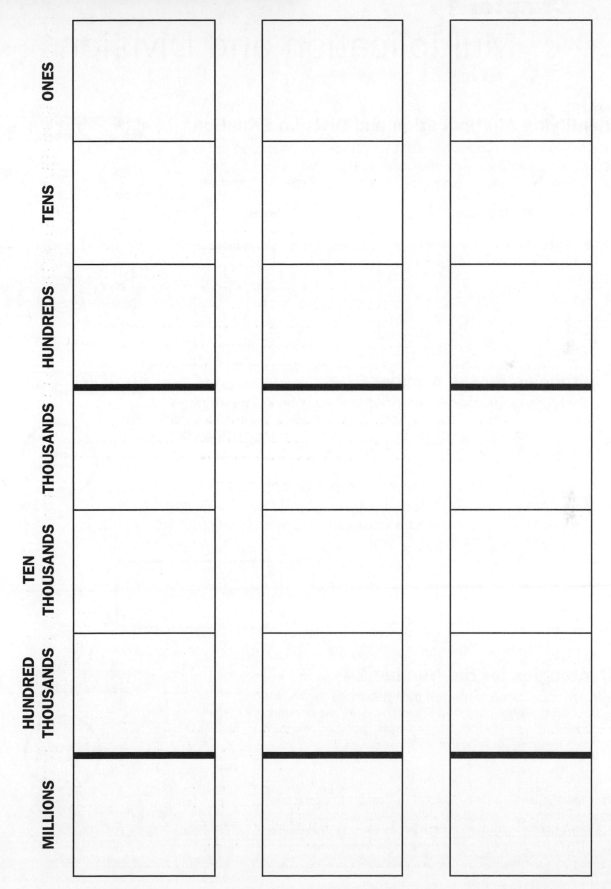

# Chapter 4
# Multiplication and Division

## 1. Identifying Multiplication and Division Situations

Standards 1, 8, 9

Brainstorm situations in your daily life in which you use multiplication and division. (Think about recess, class supplies and activities, cooking and eating, after-school games and sports.) Record the your findings below.

| Multiplication | Division |
|---|---|
| **Example:** fitting 4 rows of 4 cookies on a baking sheet | dividing up the cookies between 2 people |

## 2. Rectangles for the Number 6

Standards 1, 3, 10

Look at the rectangle marked Figure 1 on the Multiplication Squares page. The rectangle is formed by 1 square across and 6 squares down, so we can write 1 x 6 = 6 to describe it. Turn the rectangle so it is 6 squares across and 1 square down. How does the multiplication sentence change?

_____

Cut apart the Figure 1 squares. Rearrange them to form 2 new rectangles for the number 6. Draw your new rectangles below and write a multiplication sentence next to each drawing.

copy page 43

## 3. Rectangles for the Number 24

Standards 1, 3, 10

Write the multiplication sentence that describes the rectangle in Figure 2 on the Multiplication Squares page. When writing the multiplication sentence, first write the number of squares across and then the number of squares down.

_____

Cut out the Figure 2 rectangle and cut apart the squares. Rearrange them to form as many different rectangles for the number 24 as you can. On a piece of graph paper, draw what each rectangle looks like and write a multiplication sentence below each drawing.

copy page 43

Write multiplication sentences for 3 of the new rectangles you made.

_____  _____  _____

## 4. Using Mental Math to Find a Product

Standards **1, 6**

On their vacation, the Anderson family used 5 rolls of film taking pictures. Each roll of film had 24 pictures on it. Mrs. Anderson wants to know how many photos they took in all. Using mental math, figure out how many pictures the Andersons took.

_____ pictures

Explain how you solved this problem using mental math.

## 5. Exploring the Effects of Doubling Amounts

Standards **1, 7**

Suppose you were willing to take just 1 penny as an allowance this week, as long as the amount would double each week. For example, this week you would get 1¢, next week 2¢, the following week 4¢, and so on. Make a table to show what your allowance would be each week for 12 weeks.

| Week 1 = $.01 | Week 5 = | Week 9 = |
|---|---|---|
| Week 2 = | Week 6 = | Week 10 = |
| Week 3 = | Week 7 = | Week 11 = |
| Week 4 = | Week 8 = | Week 12 = |

How much allowance would you have received in all?

## 6. Exploring More Effects of Doubling Amounts

Standards **1, 7**

Suppose your allowance was $3.00 a week. If you saved each week's allowance, how much allowance would you have by the end of 12 weeks?

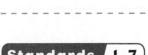Show your work:

_____

How does the total amount of allowance you receive in 12 weeks compare with the total amount of allowance in problem 5?

_____

What would be the difference in the Week 14 allowances?

_____

## 7. Comparing Smile Statistics

The average person smiles about 15 times a day.

How many times would that be in a week? _____

A month? _____    A year? _____

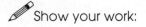 Show your work:

**Bonus:** Start a tally of the number of smiles you see at lunch over the course of 2 minutes. Then figure out how many smiles you might expect in a half hour.

## 8. Solving a Multistep Problem

"Ooh," moaned Ms. Martinez, "I have so many papers to grade!" Each child in her class (except for 2 students who were absent) had turned in 15 worksheets. There are 27 students in her class. How many papers does Ms. Martinez have to grade?

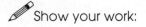 Show your work:

## 9. Solving a Multistep Problem

Mrs. Lee decided that each member of her family should eat 3 fruits and 2 vegetables each day. There are 4 people in her family. She will buy apples, oranges, bananas, carrots, and potatoes this week. How many of each does she need to buy? How many fruits and vegetables is that in all? Fill in the chart to answer the questions.

| Food Item | # Needed each day | # Needed each week |
|-----------|-------------------|--------------------|
|           |                   |                    |
|           |                   |                    |
|           |                   |                    |
|           |                   |                    |
|           |                   |                    |
| TOTAL     |                   |                    |

## 10. Comparing Estimated and Actual Products

a. Describe a way to multiply 80 x 20 using mental math.

_____

b. Round each factor to the nearest 10 and estimate the product for each of the following:

49 x 25 _____     88 x 69 _____     57 x 66 _____

c. Is each estimate in b greater than or less than the actual product? Explain.

_____

---

## 11. Draw a Picture to Solve a Multiplication Problem

Standards **1, 8, 9, 10**

Draw a picture to solve this problem:

On a street there are 4 houses. In each house there are 6 rooms. In each room are 3 pieces of furniture. How many rooms did you draw?

_____

How many pieces of furniture?

_____

---

## 12. Multiplying Ingredients in a Recipe

Standards **1, 2, 6, 9**

Molly gathered the ingredients she needed to make one of her famous breakfast sandwiches. She got 1 egg, 1 slice of cheese, half a piece of ham, 2 slices of tomato, and 2 pieces of bread. Then her sister and brother asked her to fix each of them a breakfast sandwich. How much of each ingredient does Molly need to make 3 breakfast sandwiches?

 Show your work:

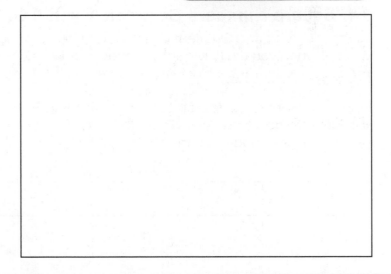

## 13. Identifying Square Numbers

Standards **1, 2, 3, 7, 10**

If you had 25 squares, you could make 1 large square (5 squares x 5 squares). The number 25 is a square number. Use the squares from the rectangle in Figure 2 on the Multiplication Squares page to find the number between 12 and 20 that is a square number. Write a multiplication sentence to describe the large square you made.

_____

Now, find two square numbers that are less than 10. Write a multiplication sentence for each one.

_____

_____

## 14. Square Numbers Between 1 and 144

Standards **1, 2**

Use the Product and Quotient Chart. Color in the product you get when you multiply each number from 1 to 12 by itself. For example, 1 x 1 = 1, color in the number 1 in the 1 column; 2 x 2 = 4, color in the number 4 in the 2 column, and so on. Remember, when two factors are the same number, the product is a square number. What pattern do you see when you color in the square numbers in the chart?

_____

_____

## 15. Identifying Prime Numbers

Standards **1, 7**

You can make only two rectangles with 5 squares, a 1 x 5 rectangle and a 5 x 1 rectangle. The number 5 is a prime number. Each prime number has only two factors, itself and 1. Make a list of all the prime numbers between 1 and 25. You can use the squares from Figure 2 on the Multiplication Squares page to help.

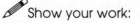 Show your work:

_____

**Hint!** You should find nine prime numbers!

## 16. Numbers Divisible by 2

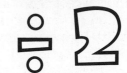

Write the numbers from 15 to 30. Divide each one by 2. Complete this sentence:

Numbers that can be divided by 2 with no remainder are

all _____ numbers.

 Show your work:

---

## 17. Numbers Divisible by 3

If a number is divisible by 3, it can be divided by 3, and there will be no remainder. Here is a way to check whether a number is divisible by 3:

a. Add all the digits that form the number (131: 1 + 3 + 1 = 5).

b. If the sum is a number that is divisible by 3, then the original number is divisible by 3 (5 is not divisible by 3; therefore, 131 is not divisible by 3.)

Complete the chart to find out which numbers are divisible by 3.

| # | Sum of digits | Divisible by 3? | Check |
|---|---|---|---|
| 54 | | | |
| 132 | | | |
| 516 | | | |

---

## 18. Numbers Divisible by 4

Roberto says that if the last two digits of a number form a number divisible by 4, then the number itself is divisible by 4. He used 732 as an example:

"The last two digits of 732 are 32; 32 is divisible by 4, so 732 is divisible by 4. 732 divided by 4 is 183."

Write 5 numbers in which the last two digits make a number divisible by 4. See if Roberto's rule works every time.

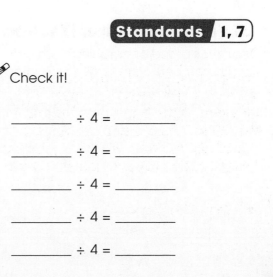 Check it!

_____ ÷ 4 = _____

_____ ÷ 4 = _____

_____ ÷ 4 = _____

_____ ÷ 4 = _____

_____ ÷ 4 = _____

## 19. Numbers Divisible by 5

**Standards 1, 2, 8**

The numbers 5, 10, 15, and 20 are multiples of 5. Write the next 10 multiples of 5.

5, 10, 15, 20, _____, _____, _____, _____, _____,

_____, _____, _____, _____, _____

What pattern do you notice?

Every number that is a multiple of 5 is also divisible by 5. Write a rule to describe how to tell if a number is divisible by 5.

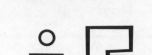

---

## 20. Numbers Divisible by 9

**Standards 1, 2**

The numbers 36, 45, 54, 63, 72, 81, 90, 99, and 108 are all divisible by 9. Write six more numbers that are divisible by 9.

_____, _____, _____, _____, _____, _____

Look at the numbers. Write a rule for identifying when a number is divisible by 9.

---

## 21. Division With a Fraction Remainder

**Standards 1, 6**

Matt was proud of catching 7 fish on a camping trip. The 4 other members of his family all wanted some fish when they smelled it cooking over the campfire. How can Matt divide the fish so everyone gets an equal share? How much will each person get?

Show your work:

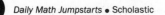

## 22. Working With Remainders

Standards **1, 6, 9**

Three classes of fifth graders are going on a field trip. Each group of 5 students needs an adult with them; therefore, in addition to their 3 teachers, some parent helpers need to go on the trip. If permission slips have been returned by 92 students and each bus seats 40 people, determine:

Show your work:

a. how many adults are needed. _____

b. how many parent helpers should be invited. _____

c. how many buses will be needed. _____

## 23. Determining the Best Buy

Standards **1, 6, 7, 9**

Tran was comparing different brands of colored pencils. He saw one set of 8 pencils for $1.99, another set of 12 pencils for $2.69, and a third set of 10 pencils for $2.39.

About how much does each pencil cost in the 8-pencil set? _____

The 12-pencil set? _____

The 10-pencil set? _____

Which set is the best buy? _____

## 24. Determining Quantity and Cost

Standards **1, 7, 9**

The students at a day-care center like fruit freezes for a snack. The freezes come in packages of 12. Each package costs $0.89. There are 234 children at the day-care center. How many packages does the day-care center need to buy so that each child gets 1 freeze?

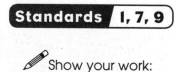

Show your work:

_____

How much will it cost to buy that many packages? Do the freezes cost more or less than $0.10 each?

_____

# Curriculum Connections

## Favorite Recipes (Nutrition)

Ask students to bring in their favorite healthy-snack recipes. They can work in small groups to increase or decrease the amounts of the ingredients in the recipes so that each recipe would make enough for the number of students in the class. If it's possible to prepare food at your school, ask students to vote to select one or two recipes to make and have them bring in the necessary ingredients. Enjoy the results!

## Old-Time Journey (Social Studies)

When cars were invented in the early 1900s, the top speed for most automobiles was about 25 miles per hour. Students can research what it must have been like on a car trip in the early twentieth century. About how long would a 100-mile drive have taken in 1920? What are some things that might have slowed down the traveler on that journey?

## Fun at the Fair (Social Studies)

In 1893, the original Ferris wheel was built for the World's Fair in Chicago. It was huge! There were 36 cars spaced around the wheel, and each car held 50 people. What is the greatest number of people that could ride on the Ferris wheel at one time? Do modern-day Ferris wheels carry more or fewer people than the original Ferris wheel? Have students research the history of other rides that they may see at amusement parks and draw pictures or write paragraphs of how the rides have changed over the years.

# Multiplication Squares

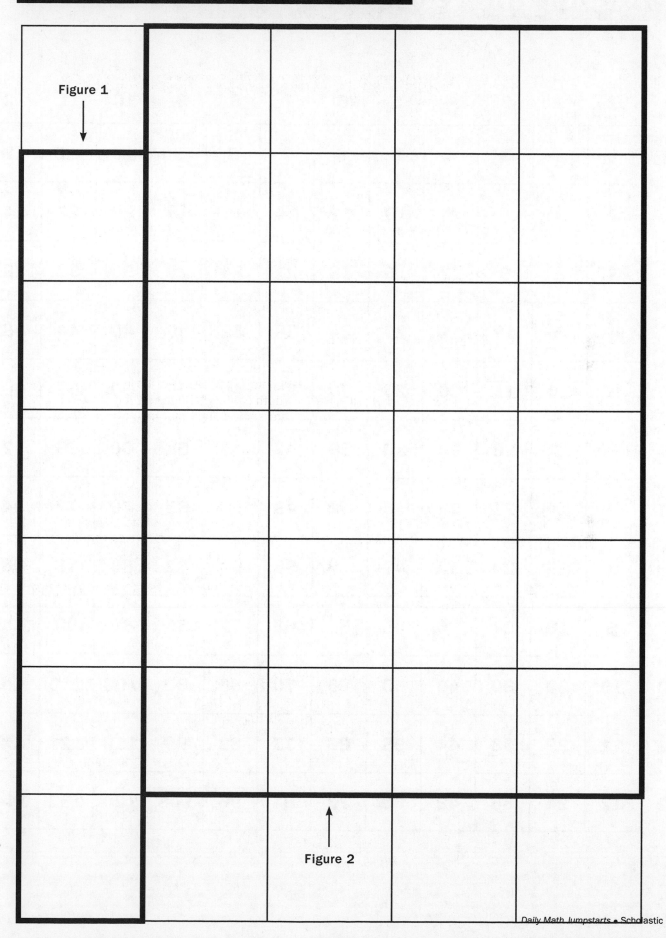

Figure 1

Figure 2

# Product and Quotient Chart

| X | 1 | 2 | 3 | 4 | 5 | 6 | 7 | 8 | 9 | 10 | 11 | 12 |
|---|---|---|---|---|---|---|---|---|---|---|---|---|
| 1 | 1 | 2 | 3 | 4 | 5 | 6 | 7 | 8 | 9 | 10 | 11 | 12 |
| 2 | 2 | 4 | 6 | 8 | 10 | 12 | 14 | 16 | 18 | 20 | 22 | 24 |
| 3 | 3 | 6 | 9 | 12 | 15 | 18 | 21 | 24 | 27 | 30 | 33 | 36 |
| 4 | 4 | 8 | 12 | 16 | 20 | 24 | 28 | 32 | 36 | 40 | 44 | 48 |
| 5 | 5 | 10 | 15 | 20 | 25 | 30 | 35 | 40 | 45 | 50 | 55 | 60 |
| 6 | 6 | 12 | 18 | 24 | 30 | 36 | 42 | 48 | 54 | 60 | 66 | 72 |
| 7 | 7 | 14 | 21 | 28 | 35 | 42 | 49 | 56 | 63 | 70 | 77 | 84 |
| 8 | 8 | 16 | 24 | 32 | 40 | 48 | 56 | 64 | 72 | 80 | 88 | 96 |
| 9 | 9 | 18 | 27 | 36 | 45 | 54 | 63 | 72 | 81 | 90 | 99 | 108 |
| 10 | 10 | 20 | 30 | 40 | 50 | 60 | 70 | 80 | 90 | 100 | 110 | 120 |
| 11 | 11 | 22 | 33 | 44 | 55 | 66 | 77 | 88 | 99 | 110 | 121 | 132 |
| 12 | 12 | 24 | 36 | 48 | 60 | 72 | 84 | 96 | 108 | 120 | 132 | 144 |

# Chapter 5
# Patterns and Codes

## 1. Drawing and Extending a Pattern

Standards 2, 3

Draw 9 triangles and color:

a. the 2nd and 6th triangles purple.

b. all the odd triangles yellow.

c. the 4th and 8th triangles red.

✏ Triangle pattern:

If the pattern continues, what color will the 10th triangle be?

_____

Add the 10th triangle to the pattern. Then continue it for 3 more triangles.

## 2. Identifying and Extending Patterns

Standards 1, 2

a. Describe this pattern and write the next 3 numbers:

37, 35, 33, 31, _____, _____, _____

b. Describe this pattern and write the next 3 numbers:

35, 38, 41, 44, 47, _____, _____, _____

c. Combine the patterns in **a** and **b** to create a new pattern, following these steps:

1. Start with 35.
2. Use the pattern in **a** to write the next number.
3. Use the pattern in **b** to write the next number.
4. Repeat, alternating between the **a** pattern and the **b** pattern.
5. What are the first 5 numbers in the new pattern?

35, _____, _____, _____, _____

## 3. Extending Patterns From Memory

Standards 2, 3, 8

Look at the pattern in Figure 1 on the Patterns page for 30 seconds. Turn the page over so you can't see the shapes and try to picture the pattern in your mind. Look at the pattern again for 10 seconds. Then turn the page over. From memory, draw the next 3 shapes in the pattern. Compare your drawing to Figure 1.

copy page 52

## 4. Extending Patterns From Memory Again

copy
page 52

**Standards** 2, 3, 8

Look at the pattern in Figure 2 on the Patterns page for 30 seconds. Turn the page over so you can't see the shapes. Close your eyes and try to picture the pattern in your mind. Look at the pattern again for 10 seconds. Then turn the page over. From memory, draw the next row in the pattern. Compare your drawing to Figure 2.

---

## 5. Creating a Pattern

**Standards** 1, 2, 6, 8

Kenisha plans to make 5 beaded bracelets to give as gifts. She buys 50 white beads, 25 blue beads, and 25 red beads. The 5 bracelets will have the same pattern and number of beads. How many of the following beads will Kenisha use in each bracelet?

White beads _____    Blue beads _____    Red beads _____

Draw or describe a pattern to show how Kenisha could string together all the beads in one bracelet.

---

## 6. Finding a Pattern to Solve a Problem

**Standards** 1, 2, 6, 7

Jake and Jody went on a camping trip. On Monday, they saw some tents near their campsite. On Tuesday, they saw twice as many tents as the day before, and on Wednesday, 3 times as many tents as on Monday. On Thursday, they saw 8 tents—2 more than on Wednesday. Friday, they saw 2 more tents than on Thursday, which was 5 times as many as on Monday.

Describe the pattern by completing the table. If the pattern continues, how many tents will Jake and Jody see on Saturday?

| Day of the Week | | | | | |
|---|---|---|---|---|---|
| **Number of Tents** | | | | | |

## 7. Rotating Schedules

Standards 2, 6, 7, 9

At Mathville Elementary, the weekly specialist schedule goes Art, Technology, P.E, Library and then starts over again. If the fourth grade starts with Art class on Monday, what class will they have on Friday?

_____

What will the schedule be for the following week?

| Monday | Tuesday | Wednesday | Thursday | Friday |
|--------|---------|-----------|----------|--------|
|        |         |           |          |        |

## 8. Presidential-Election Year Pattern

Standards 1, 2, 9

Every 4 years we have presidential elections. The first election of the 21st century was in November, 2000. Between 2000 and 2025, which years will be presidential election years?

2000, _____

 Show your work:

## 9. Fibonacci Sequence

Standards 1, 2, 9

There is a special pattern of numbers called the **Fibonacci sequence**, named after the man who discovered it. He studied the natural world and noticed a pattern in the numbers of things, such as petals on flowers and leaves on stems. This is how the Fibonacci sequence begins:
1, 1, 2, 3, 5, 8, 13, 21, 34

Describe the pattern. _____

What are the next 3 numbers in the Fibonacci sequence?

_____, _____, _____

## 10. Values of Roman Numerals

Standards 1, 2

Use the Roman Numeral Chart in Figure 1 to decipher the value of the following numerals:

CLXV _____

MCMXCIX _____

DXXXII _____

copy page 53

---

## 11. Using Roman Numerals

Standards 1, 2

Use the Roman Numerals Chart in Figure 1 to rewrite the following street address and phone number using numerals from our number system (1, 2, 3, and so on):

address: CLX Payson Rd. _____

phone: IX II VI–VIII VII IV I _____

Write your street address and phone number using Roman numerals. (Think of your phone number as seven separate digits.)

_____     _____

copy page 53

---

## 12. Hindu Numerals

Standards 2, 7, 8, 9

The people who invented our number system lived in India about 2,000 years ago. The system they used is called the Hindu system. The Arabs further developed the system, and eventually the symbols evolved into the numerals we use today.

Look at the Hindu Numerals chart in Figure 2. Write today's date and the date you were born (month, day, year) using the Hindu numerals.

_____

_____

copy page 53

## 13. Pictographs

Standards  1, 2, 8, 9, 10

Native Americans drew pictographs to tell stories, describe events, and record information. Pictographs use symbols for animals, people, and objects. Without using a symbol for the number 4, how could you represent 4 deer in a pictograph?

Write a sentence about yourself or your family that includes a number, for example: "Our family has 3 guinea pigs." Draw a pictograph to represent your sentence.

_____

_____

## 14. Using a Number-Letter Code

Standards  2, 8, 9

Follow these simple directions to turn words into number codes using the Code Wheel:

• Cut out the wheels.
• Poke a hole through each center dot.
• Place the smaller wheel on top of the larger one, lining up the holes.
• Put a brass paper fastener through the holes to keep the wheels together.

copy page 54

Turn your code wheel so the number 8 lines up with the letter A. To record the number code for the word *hat*, write the numbers that line up with the letters *H, A,* and *T*. What is the number code for hat?

\_\_\_\_\_-\_\_\_\_\_-\_\_\_\_\_

Keep the number 8 lined up with the letter A on your code wheel. Write the number code for *Math is great!*

\_\_\_\_\_-\_\_\_\_\_-\_\_\_\_\_-\_\_\_\_\_  \_\_\_\_\_-\_\_\_\_\_  \_\_\_\_\_-\_\_\_\_\_-\_\_\_\_\_-\_\_\_\_\_-\_\_\_\_\_!

## 15. Using a Number-Letter Code

Standards  2, 8, 9

Follow the directions in number 14 to construct a Code Wheel. Then decode this sentence. (Hint: 23–7 is the number code for the word is.)

copy page 54

8–3–18–15–13     23–7     13–3–9–6     26–9–17–25–13     18–15–13!

_____     \_\_\_\_\_     _____     _____     _____!

## 16. Creating a Code

Standards 2, 6, 8, 9

Assemble your Code Wheels (see the directions in number 14) to make up your own code. You can write numbers for letters, or you can use other symbols. Write a sentence using your code. Then write a key that describes how to decode it.

copy
page 54

_____

_____

| Key |
| --- |
|  |
|  |
|  |
|  |

---

## 17. Finding Your Lucky Number

Standards 1, 2, 9

Here's a way to find a number some people believe to be a lucky number:

• Write down your birth date using numbers (month, day, and year).

• Find the sum of all the digits. For example, 5/11/1998 would be

$$5 + 1 + 1 + 1 + 9 + 9 + 8 = 34.$$

• Add the digits of the 2-digit number together. If the sum is a 2-digit number, add those digits together. Repeat until you get a 1-digit number. That's your lucky number!

Your birth date number sum _____

Your lucky number _____

---

## 18. Shape, Number, and Color Patterns in the Classroom

Standards 2, 3, 8, 9

There are probably many shape, number, and color patterns in your classroom. For example, the ceiling tiles could have patterns of dots. That is a shape pattern. The calendar may show the numbers 7, 14, 21, 28 in one column. That is a number pattern. The bulletin board could have a blue and white border around it. That is a color pattern.

Find a shape, a number, and a color pattern in your classroom. Draw a picture or write a description of each one.

Shape pattern:          Number pattern:          Color pattern:

# Curriculum Connections

## Patterns in Poetry (Language Arts)

Poems often have sound patterns created by rhyme and rhythm. Write on the board a simple poem such as the following:

> Jack and Jill went up a hill,
> To fetch a pail of water.
> Jack fell down and broke his crown,
> And Jill came tumbling after.

Have students read the poem aloud and identify the pairs of rhyming words (*Jill*, *hill*; *down*, *crown*; *water*, *after*). Ask them to read the poem again, clapping softly to identify the rhythm in each line.

Pair students, and ask them to write a short poem. Encourage pairs to read aloud their poems so the other students can identify the rhyme and rhythm patterns.

## Musical Patterns (Music)

Explain that manufactured objects often exhibit the Fibonacci proportions. Use piano keys as an example (although there are 88 instead of 89 keys): there are clusters of 2 black keys above 3 white keys and 3 black keys above 5 white keys; octaves are made up of 8 keys.

Invite the music teacher or a volunteer musician to demonstrate and discuss patterns in music with students.

## Sound and Movement Patterns (Music, Sports, and Recreation)

Rhythm is very important to dancers and musicians. It is conveyed in the pattern of sounds in music and the pattern of movement in dance. Have students work together in small groups to create a rhythm using sound (tapping, clapping, or stamping) or a rhythm using movement. Let each group demonstrate their sound or movement pattern and teach it to the rest of the class.

## Ancient Stories (Social Studies)

Have students research how the ancient Romans, Hindus, or Native Americans lived and what kind of number system them used. Tell them to write word problems incorporating their research information—including the numerals and other symbols they learned about in this chapter or in their research.

# Patterns

**Figure 1**

**Figure 2**

# Ancient Numeration Systems

Figure 1

| Roman Numerals | | | |
|---|---|---|---|
| 1 | I | 8 | VIII |
| 2 | II | 9 | IX |
| 3 | III | 10 | X |
| 4 | IV | 50 | L |
| 5 | V | 100 | C |
| 6 | VI | 500 | D |

Figure 2

| Hindu Numerals | | | |
|---|---|---|---|
| 1 | — | 6 |  76 |
| 2 | = | 7 |  7 |
| 3 | ≡ | 8 |  y |
| 4 |  4 | 9 |  ? |
| 5 |  5 | 10 |  α |

# Code Wheel

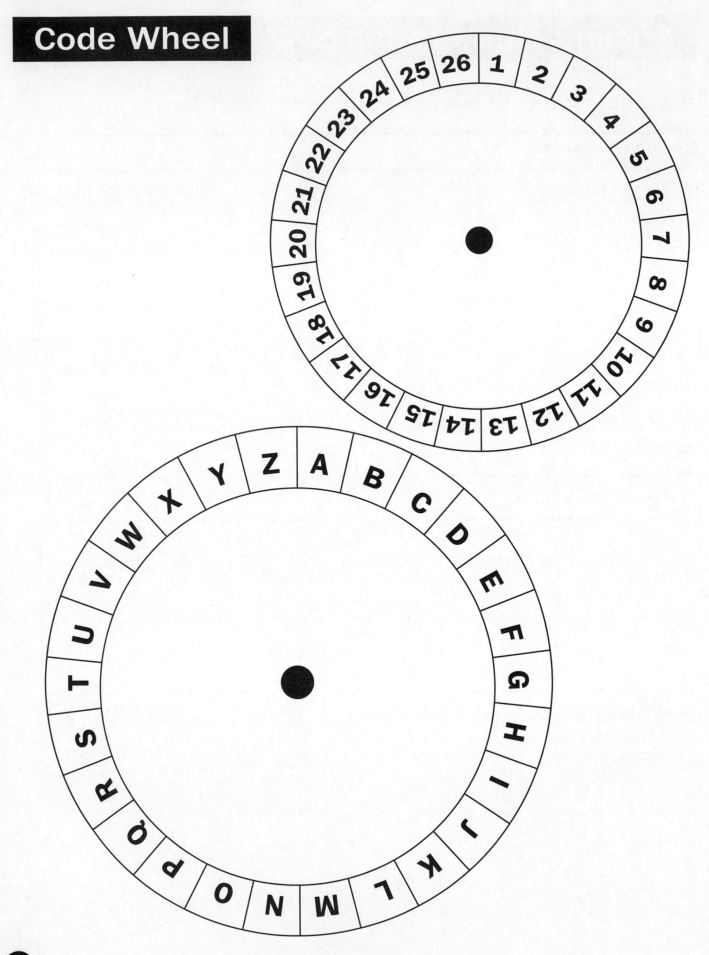

# Chapter 6
# Fractions, Decimals and Percents

## 1. Paper Folding: Halves

Standards 1, 3, 10

Fold a sheet of paper in half. How many sections do you have when you unfold it? _____

Now predict how many sections you think you will have if you fold a sheet of paper in half and then in half again. _____ What if you fold it in half a third time? _____

Fold the paper to check your predictions and fill in the chart. Will the number of sections be the same with paper of any size and shape? _____

| Fold # | Sections |
|--------|----------|
|        |          |
|        |          |
|        |          |

## 2. Things That Can and Can't Be Divided in Half

Standards 1, 3, 9

List 3 things that would be just as good if you cut them in half.

1.

2.

3.

List 3 things that would be ruined if you cut them in half.

1.

2.

3.

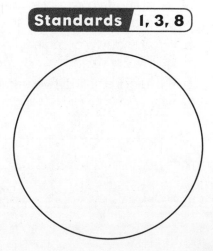

## 3. Applying the Concept of One-Third

Standards 1, 3, 8

Divide the circle into 3 equal sections. Shade 1 section. The fraction ⅓ describes the shaded part. Write a story problem that has the fraction ⅓ in it.

_____

_____

_____

_____

## 4. Fractions Equal to 1

Standards **1, 8, 10**

Cut out each fraction strip. Then cut along the dotted lines to cut each strip into equal sections. You should have two ½ sections, three ⅓ sections, four ¼ sections, and so on.

Cover up the strip representing 1 whole (labeled with 1) with a combination of strips that have 3 different denominators. Record each combination below by writing a number sentence, for example, ½ + ¼ + ⅛ + ⅛ = 1.

copy
page 63

1. _____

2. _____

3. _____

---

## 5. Comparing Fractions

Standards **1, 10**

Cut apart each fraction strip to help compare fractions. Pick 2 fraction strips and compare them. Record below four different comparisons using **>**, **<**, or **=**.

copy
page 63

1. _____

2. _____

3. _____

4. _____

---

## 6. Finding Equivalent Fractions

Standards **1, 8, 10**

Cut out each fraction strip. Follow these steps to find equivalent fractions:

a. Choose a fraction strip.

b. Try to find two or more fraction strips that when placed together are equivalent, or equal to, the first fraction strip.

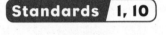

copy
page 63

c. If you find two or more strips that are equivalent, record them in a number senter below. For example, ⅛ + ¹⁄₁₆ + ¹⁄₁₆ = ¼.

d. If you cannot find two or more strips that are equivalent, record the original fraction and write, *no equivalent sections found.*

1. _____  4. _____

2. _____  5. _____

3. _____

## 7. Comparing Non-Unit Fractions

Use what you know about fractions to write the following fractions in order from least to greatest: ⁴/₅, ³/₄, ⁷/₈, ²/₃.

_____, _____, _____, _____

Describe one way you could check your answer.

_____

_____

## 8. Adding Fractions

**Standards / 1, 2, 6, 9**

Kiko has a little dog, Shadow, and Sophie has a very big dog, Rolly. Shadow eats ⅓ as much as Rolly. Rolly eats 1 bag of dog food each week. Complete the table to find the answers to these questions:

How much does Shadow eat each week?

_____

How much does Rolly eat in 8 weeks?

_____

How much does Shadow eat in 8 weeks?

_____

| Week | Bags of Food | |
| --- | --- | --- |
| | Rolly | Shadow |
| 1 | 1 | ⅓ |
| 2 | 2 | ⅔ |
| 3 | 3 | 1 |
| 4 | 4 | 1⅓ |
| 5 | | |
| 6 | | |
| 7 | | |
| 8 | | |

## 9. Fractions Equal to 1

**Standards / 1, 6, 8**

Juan, Jaime, and Joel are brothers who worked together to paint a fence. Juan, who is the oldest, said he'd paint half the fence. Jaime, the middle brother, said he'd paint one third of the fence. Joel, the youngest, would paint whatever part was left. How much of the fence did each brother paint?

Juan _____   Jamie _____   Joel _____

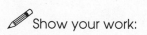 Show your work:

## 10. Fraction of a Number

Cyrus and his dad are making spaghetti for dinner. The recipe makes enough spaghetti for 12 people, but they only need to make enough for ¼ of that number. For how many people are they making spaghetti?

New List:

_____

This is the ingredient list for the recipe:

4 cans tomato sauce
2 cans tomato paste
8 cups chopped tomatoes
4 pounds of spaghetti

Rewrite the ingredient list so Cyrus and his dad will have the exact amount of each ingredient they need.

## 11. Dividing a Lesser Number by a Greater Number

Suppose you have 3 friends over to play, and everybody (including you) wants a snack. But there are only 3 cupcakes. How much of a cupcake will each person get?

_____

Draw a picture to help solve this problem!

## 12. A Fraction of a Fraction

Draw a picture to show that ¼ of ½ is the same as ½ of ¼.

## 13. Finding Half of a Fraction

Standards | 1, 3, 6, 7, 8

Devon and Troy decide to combine their money to buy a pizza. Troy has only half as much money as Devon, so he is only going to eat half as much pizza. How much of the pizza will each one eat?

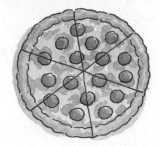

Devon's piece _____     Troy's piece _____

Show your work:

---

## 14. Ratios

Standards | 1, 2, 3, 10

Make two designs showing diamonds and triangles in a 1 to 4 ratio; that is, for each diamond you draw, draw 4 triangles. Each drawing should include a different number of triangles and diamonds, but it should represent the same ratio (1 to 4). Below each drawing, write the ratio it represents.

| Design 1 | Design 2 |
|---|---|
| | |
| Ratio _____ | Ratio _____ |

---

## 15. Places Where Decimals Are Used

Standards | 1, 4, 9

Often decimals are used instead of fractions to show amounts less than 1, or amounts between whole numbers. Name two places where decimals are used, and give three examples of the decimals that might be used there.

1. _____ : _____ , _____ , _____

2. _____ : _____ , _____ , _____

## 16. Writing Decimals

**Standards 1, 6, 7**

Tina is going to use the digits 5, 9, 2, 7, 4, 1 to write decimals. The only rule is she must have at least 1 digit on either side of the decimal point.

What is the greatest possible decimal Tina can write using all the digits?

__________________

What is the least possible decimal Tina can write using all the digits?

__________________

## 17. Drawing to Show Equivalent Fractions and Decimals

**Standards 1, 3, 8, 10**

Use the Fractions and Decimals page. In Section 1, color in $\frac{1}{4}$ of the top square and 0.25 of the bottom square. What do you notice?

In Section 2, color in $\frac{2}{5}$ of the top square. Color the bottom square to show the decimal equivalent to $\frac{2}{5}$. What is the decimal? ________

In Section 3, color in $\frac{1}{3}$ of the top square. Color the bottom square to show the decimal equivalent to $\frac{1}{3}$. What is the decimal? ________

In Section 4, color in $\frac{6}{8}$ of the top square. Color the bottom square to show the decimal equivalent to $\frac{6}{8}$. What is the decimal? ________

## 18. Finding Percents

**Standards 1, 6**

If 20% of the people in a city drive red cars, what percentage of people in the city do not drive red cars?

________

Make up a problem of your own that has an answer of 60%.

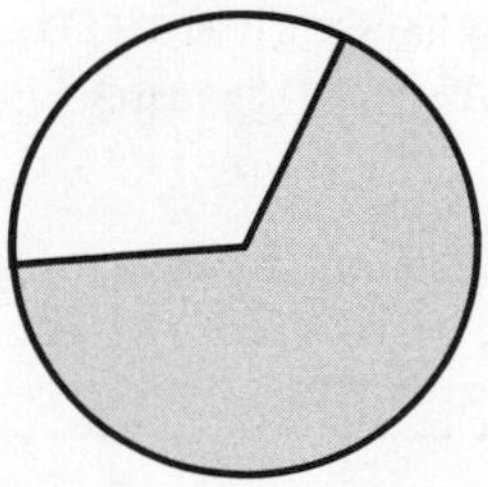

## 19. Drawing to Show Percents

Standards | 1, 8, 10

Label each of the four squares made up of 100 smaller squares on the Fractions and Decimals page **a**, **b**, **c**, or **d**. Then draw the following:

a. a design with 30% colored blue

b. the letter L so that it covers 14% of the square

c. a design with 25% colored yellow and 75% colored green

d. a house that covers 60% of the square

copy
page 64

## 20. Writing Percents and Fractions as Decimals

Standards | 1, 9

There is a lot of water in the food we eat. A watermelon is 98% water. A potato is ¾ water. An apple is ⅘ water. Write these foods in order from the least amount of water to the greatest amount. (Remember, ¾ means the same as 3 ÷ 4.)

1. _____

2. _____

3. _____

⅘ water

## 21. Adding and Multiplying Decimals

Standards | 1, 6, 9

Bobby is earning money for a charity by doing a walk-a-thon. For every tenth of a mile he walks, he earns a quarter for the charity. The first hour Bobby walked 2.3 miles. The second hour he walked 2.9 miles. The third hour Bobby walked 3.1 miles, and the fourth hour he walked 1.8 miles.

✎ Show your work:

How many miles did Bobby walk?

_____

How much money did he earn?

_____

# Curriculum Connections

## Fraction Feast (Nutrition)

Ask students to bring in food items that can be cut into many equal pieces. Some possible items are fruits such as bananas and apples, brownies—or anything else baked in a rectangular pan—tortillas, cheese, and, of course, pizza. Discuss the variety of the shapes and sizes of the food. As each food item is cut into equal pieces, discuss the fractions represented. For example, if an apple is cut into 6 wedges, one wedge represents ⅙ of the apple, 2 wedges ⅓ of the apple, and so on.

## Enlarging a Drawing (Art)

Have students use the reproducible on page 65 to enlarge the drawing of the elephant using a 1:3 ratio. Explain that each part of the elephant drawn on the small grid will be drawn 3 times larger on the big grid. Instruct them to draw what is in each square of the small grid in the corresponding square of the big grid, beginning with the square in the top left-hand corner.

# Fraction Strips

| 1 | | | | | | | | | | | | | | | |
|---|---|---|---|---|---|---|---|---|---|---|---|---|---|---|---|

| ½ | | | | | | | | ½ | | | | | | | |

| ¼ | | | | ¼ | | | | ¼ | | | | ¼ | | | |

| ⅛ | | ⅛ | | ⅛ | | ⅛ | | ⅛ | | ⅛ | | ⅛ | | ⅛ | |

| ¹⁄₁₆ | ¹⁄₁₆ | ¹⁄₁₆ | ¹⁄₁₆ | ¹⁄₁₆ | ¹⁄₁₆ | ¹⁄₁₆ | ¹⁄₁₆ | ¹⁄₁₆ | ¹⁄₁₆ | ¹⁄₁₆ | ¹⁄₁₆ | ¹⁄₁₆ | ¹⁄₁₆ | ¹⁄₁₆ | ¹⁄₁₆ |

| $\frac{1}{12}$ | $\frac{1}{12}$ | $\frac{1}{12}$ | $\frac{1}{12}$ | $\frac{1}{12}$ | $\frac{1}{12}$ | $\frac{1}{12}$ | $\frac{1}{12}$ | $\frac{1}{12}$ | $\frac{1}{12}$ | $\frac{1}{12}$ | $\frac{1}{12}$ |

| ⅓ | | | | ⅓ | | | | ⅓ | | | |

| ⅙ | | ⅙ | | ⅙ | | ⅙ | | ⅙ | | ⅙ | |

| ⅑ | ⅑ | ⅑ | ⅑ | ⅑ | ⅑ | ⅑ | ⅑ | ⅑ |

| ⅕ | | ⅕ | | ⅕ | | ⅕ | | ⅕ | |

# Fractions and Decimals

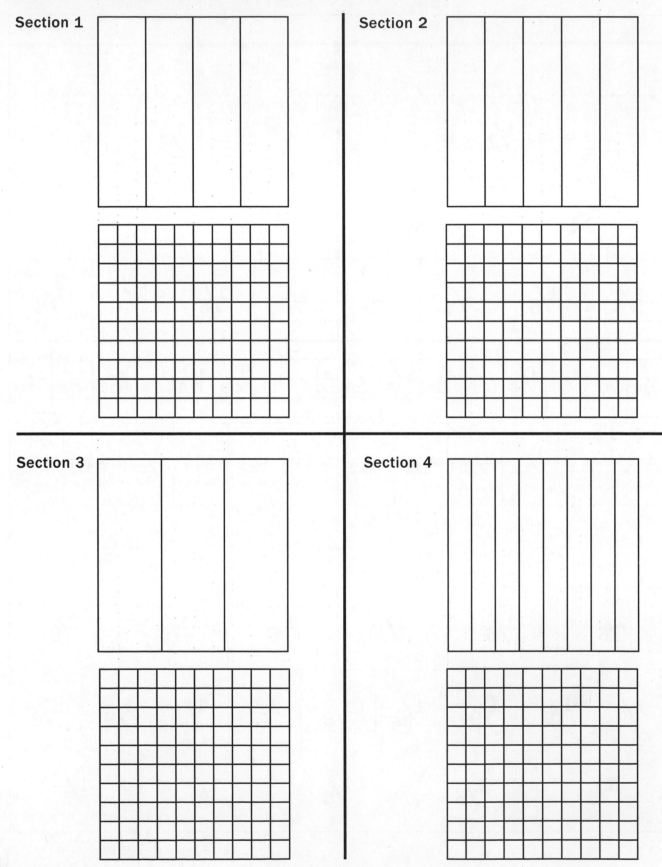

Section 1

Section 2

Section 3

Section 4

# Enlarging a Drawing

*Hint:* Draw what is in each square of the small grid in the corresponding square of the big grid. Begin with the square in the top left corner.

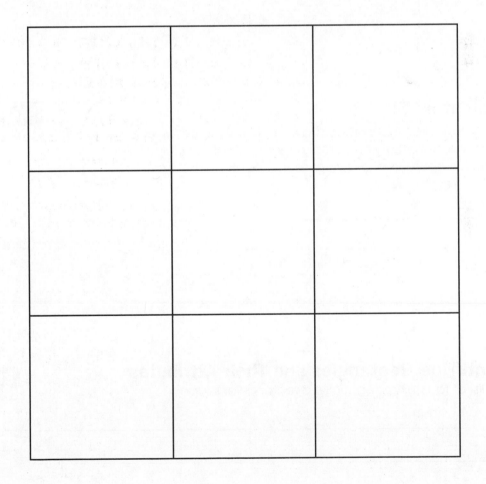

# Chapter 7
# Geometry and Spatial Awareness

## 1. Identifying Shapes and Estimating Sizes

**Standards** 3, 4, 8, 10

Draw and label as many things as you can that are about the same shape as a quarter. Estimate whether each one is smaller or larger than a quarter. Compare the items to the quarter below to check your estimates.

## 2. Estimating Size

**Standards** 3, 4, 8

On a separate piece of paper, draw the following items from memory (no looking!), trying to make them actual size: paper clip, pen, ruler. Compare your drawings to the real items. How did you do in estimating the sizes?

_____

_____

## 3. Identifying Rectangles and Their Attributes

**Standards** 3, 9

Make a list of four things that have a rectangular shape.

1. _____   2. _____

3. _____   4. _____

Describe two ways in which all rectangles are the same.

1. _____

2. _____

## 4. Identifying a Shape From Its Description

Standards 3, 4, 7

Look at the 4-sided shapes in Figure 1 on the Shapes page. Write the number of the shape that fits each of the following descriptions:

a. Each of its corners is a square corner, or right angle.

_____

b. Two of the sides are twice as long as the other 2 sides.

_____

c. Exactly 1 pair of parallel segments forms 2 of the sides.

_____

## 5. Describing and Identifying Shapes

Standards 3, 4, 7, 8

Write a description of the shapes in Figure 1. You cannot mention the name of the shape; however, you can describe the sides as slanted or straight, the lengths of sides, sizes of angles, and so on. Give only two clues per shape.

**Mystery Shape A**
- 
- 

**Mystery Shape B**
- 
- 

**Mystery Shape C**
- 
- 

**Mystery Shape D**
- 
- 

## 6. Drawing Triangles

Standards 3, 4, 8

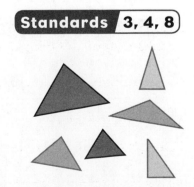

Using a ruler, draw each triangle described below. Label each triangle with the same letter as its description—a, b, or c.

a. None of the 3 sides are the same length.

b. Two of the 3 sides are the same length.

c. All 3 angles, or corners, are the same size.

## 7. Visualization: Paper Folding and Cutting

Standards 3, 7, 8, 10

copy
page 75

Suppose you fold a piece of paper in half and make 3 cuts along the fold, as shown in Figure 2. What shapes do you think you would see when you unfolded the paper? Draw your prediction.

Now, fold and cut a piece of paper as shown in Figure 2. What shapes do you see when you unfold the paper?

_____    _____    _____

How do the results compare with your predictions?

_____

## 8. Visualization: Paper Folding and Cutting

Standards 3, 7, 8, 10

Fold a piece of paper in half. Make some cuts along the fold. Predict, in writing or a drawing, what the paper will look like when you unfold it.

Unfold the paper to check your prediction.

Repeat the activity, this time folding a piece of paper in half twice.

Describe how the unfolded papers compared with your predictions.

_____

_____

## 9. Paper Folding: Sixths

Standards 1, 3, 4, 7

Divide a sheet of paper into 6 equal sections by drawing 5 lines. Divide another sheet of paper into 6 equal sections by drawing only 3 lines.

Show how you did it here:

## 10. Paper Folding: Cube

Standards 3, 7

Look at the shape in Figure 1 on the Silhouettes page. Think about how you could fold it into a cube. Test your idea by cutting out the shape and folding and taping it into a cube. Write or draw the steps you followed to make your cube.

copy page 76

## 11. Missing Angles

Standards 3, 4, 6, 7

Look at the pie and the pie pieces labeled A, B, and C in Figure 2 on the Silhouettes pages. Think of a way, other than cutting out the pie pieces and fitting them into the empty space, to tell which piece is the one missing from the pie. Try your idea. Which piece fits in the empty space?

copy page 76

_____

✏️ Explain your strategy.

## 12. Properties of Polygons

Standards 2, 3

Polygon means "many angles" in Greek. Polygons are closed figures that have 3 or more angles and 3 or more straight sides. Draw three different polygons. Identify the number of sides and angles in each one.

What do you notice about the number of angles compared to the number of sides?

_____

_____

## 13. Names of Polygons

Standards 3, 9

Write the meaning of each prefix. You can use a dictionary to help you.

copy page 77

- penta- _____
- octa- _____

- hexa- _____
- nona- _____

- hepta- _____
- deca- _____

Look at the shapes on the Polygon Card page (Page 77). Write the name of each polygon on it. Choose from the following names: pentagon, hexagon, heptagon, octagon, nonagon, and decagon.

## 14. Polygons Race

Standards 3, 8, 9

Name as many examples of polygons as you can in 2 minutes. Record the name of the polygon and the example or examples.

| Polygon | Examples |
|---|---|
| octagon | stop sign |
| | |

## 15. Shape Flash Cards

Standards 3, 8

Cut out the cards from the Polygon Card page. Write the name of the polygon on the back of each card and a hint to remember its name.

copy page 77

## 16. The Meaning of Concentric Shapes

Standards 3, 8

Concentric shapes have a common center. To draw concentric shapes, outline a large shape on a piece of blank paper. (You can draw a shape with a combination of curved and straight lines, like a square with a half circle above it, or any shape you'd like.) Draw the same outline, only smaller, inside the first outline. Continue drawing smaller and smaller outlines of the shape until you have no more room to draw. How many concentric shapes did you draw?

———

4 concentric shapes

## 17. Tessellations

Standards 3, 6, 8, 10

Tessellations are like puzzles. They are patterns made with shapes that fit together without overlapping or leaving any spaces. When shapes fit together this way, we say they tessellate.

Cut out the pentagon or hexagon shape from the Polygon Card page. Trace the polygon repeatedly. On a separate piece of paper, draw the outlines so they tessellate, or fit together like pieces of a puzzle (see problem 18 below).

copy page 77

## 18. Geometric Designs

Standards 3, 8, 10

Draw a picture or design that includes concentric shapes and tessellations. Using the names of the polygons, explain which shapes are concentric and which shapes tessellate.

concentric

tessellating

## 19. Composite Shapes

Standards 3, 7, 10

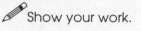

You can create shapes out of other, smaller shapes. For example, different numbers of triangles can be used to form many new shapes. Figure out how many triangles it would take to make each of the following shapes. Record your findings below.

Show your work.

| Shape | Number of Triangles |
|---|---|
| Square | |
| Rectangle | |
| Pentagon | |
| Hexagon | |
| Octagon | |

## 20. An Introduction to Tangrams

Standards 3, 8

copy page 78

Tangrams were invented by the Chinese 4,000 years ago. Legend says that a man named Tan was carrying a ceramic tile for the emperor and dropped it. However, he found many wonderful figures and designs to make while he was trying to reassemble the tile. The emperor didn't get his tile, but Tan became the famous inventor of tangrams. All tangrams are made up of 7 pieces that can fit together to form a square.

Look closely at Figure 1 on the Tangram page to see how the tangram pieces fit together. Cut out the pieces. Now put the square back together again on a piece of paper. Outline each tangram piece in the square you made to show where each piece belongs.

## 21. Describing Tangram Pieces

Standards 3, 4, 7

copy page 78

Make a list of all the shapes of the tangram pieces in Figure 1.

a. How many different shapes are there? _____

b. How many different sizes of triangles are there? _____

c. What 3 pieces, when placed together, form a triangle that matches a large triangle?

_____, _____, _____

*Hint:* Cut out the pieces of the tangram to help!

## 22. A Tangram Fox

Standards 3, 7

Look at the fox in Figure 2 on the Tangram page. Use your 7 tangram pieces to make this animal on a piece of paper. Outline each tangram piece in your fox shape to show where each piece belongs.

✎ Draw your solution.

copy
page 78

## 23. A Tangram Dog

Standards 3, 7

Change the fox you made into the dog in Figure 3 on the Tangram page by switching two pieces and turning all the other pieces in place. Outline each tangram piece in your dog shape to show where each piece belongs. Color the two pieces you switched yellow. Color the pieces you turned in place green.

✎ Draw your solution.

copy
page 78

## 24. Origami

Standards 3, 8, 9

The Japanese created origami, which is the art of paper folding. Many beautiful 3-dimensional objects can be made by folding paper. In Japan, people learn origami as young children.

To make your own origami cup follow the steps below:

1. Cut out the large square on the Origami Cup page.

2. Copy the letters A–F as they appear on the front of the square onto the back of the square too, so that when the paper is folded, you can read the letters no matter which side is showing.

3. Follow the steps shown to make the cup.

copy
page 79

**Hint:** If you'd like to be able to drink out of the cup, make it out of wax paper.

# Curriculum Connections

## Shape Poetry (Language Arts)

Have students write poems describing objects. Model how to arrange the words of the poem into the shape of the object using the example given below. Display the poems for everyone to enjoy.

all
diamonds shimmer
their light is reflected into
a thousand points of
color

## Investigate the Artists (Art)

Abstract artists use lines, shapes, and tessellations in interesting ways. Have individual students or groups research and report on artists such as M. C. Escher, Piet Mondrian, Georges Braque, Henri Matisse, and Alexander Calder.

If possible, plan a field trip to an art museum so students can see examples of the connection between math and art. In addition to abstract drawings and paintings, objects such as tapestries and vases often have patterns showing tessellations and concentric shapes.

## Paper Flowers (Art)

Brighten up the classroom with some colorful tissue- or crepe-paper flowers!

Follow the directions to make one flower:

❶ Make a stack of 4–5 square pieces of tissue or crepe paper.

❷ Fold the paper accordion style.

❸ Twist a pipe cleaner or piece of florist wire around the middle of the paper, making a "bow tie."

❹ Fluff out the layers.

# Shapes

**Figure 1**

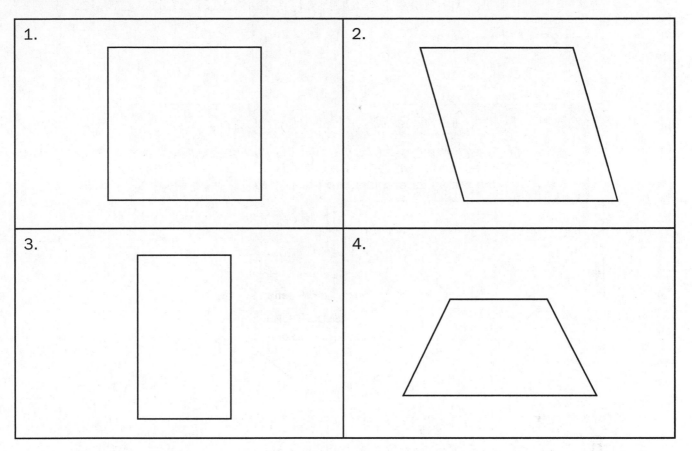

1.

2.

3.

4.

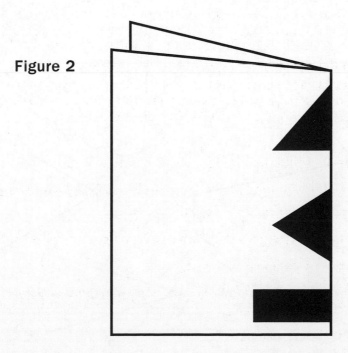

**Figure 2**

# Silhouettes

**Figure 1**

CUBE

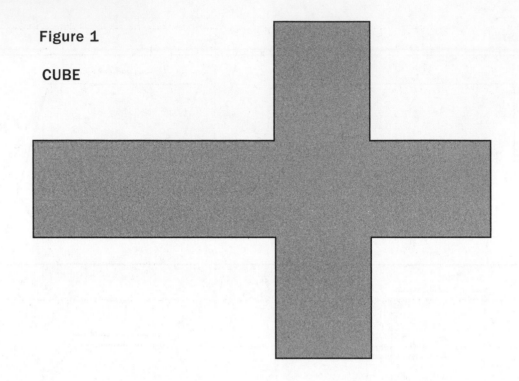

**Figure 2**

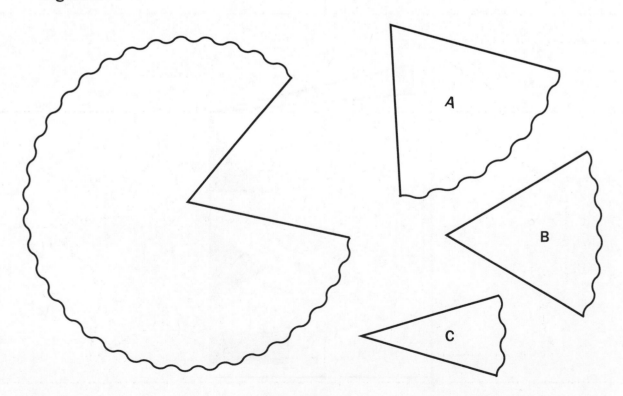

# Polygon Card

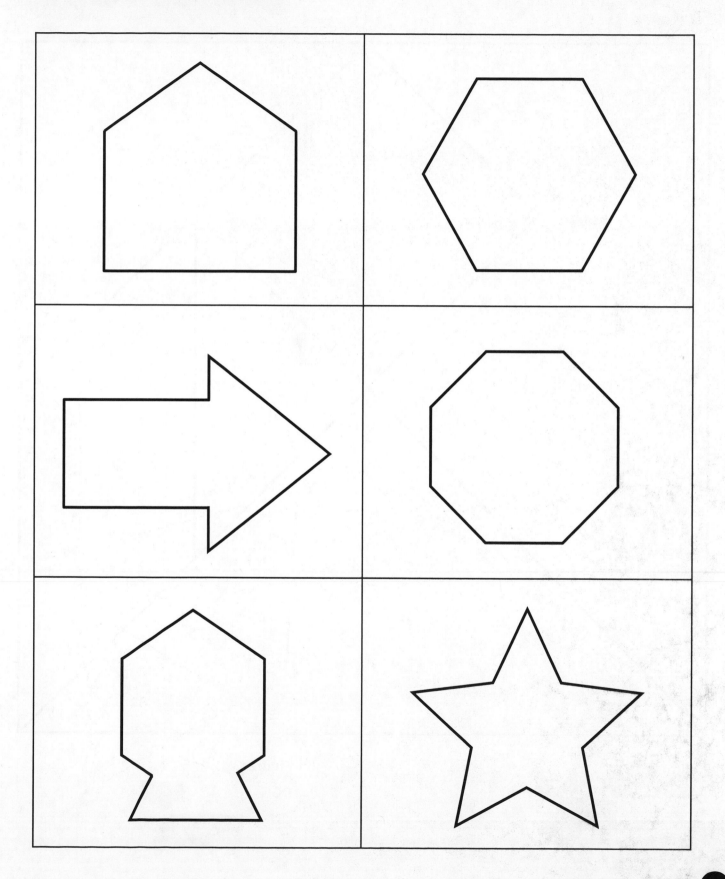

# Tangrams

**Figure 1**

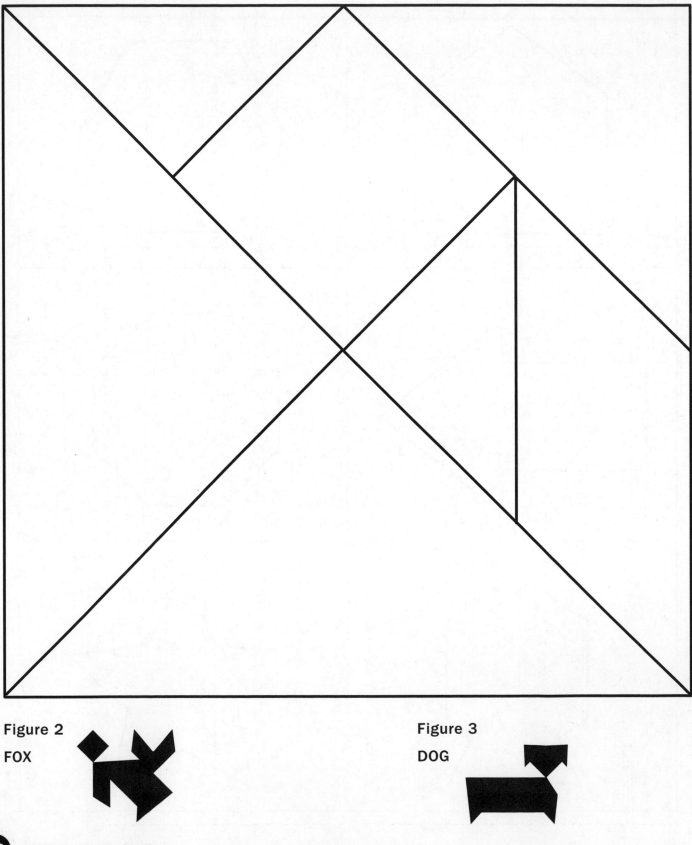

**Figure 2**

**FOX**

**Figure 3**

**DOG**

# Origami Cup

1.

A C

E

B D

Fold diagonally

2.

A

F B E

D

3.

C

E F

D

Turn over

4.

C

E D

5.

A

C

E D

Tuck into pocket

6.

A

F B

Turn over.
Tuck into pocket

7.

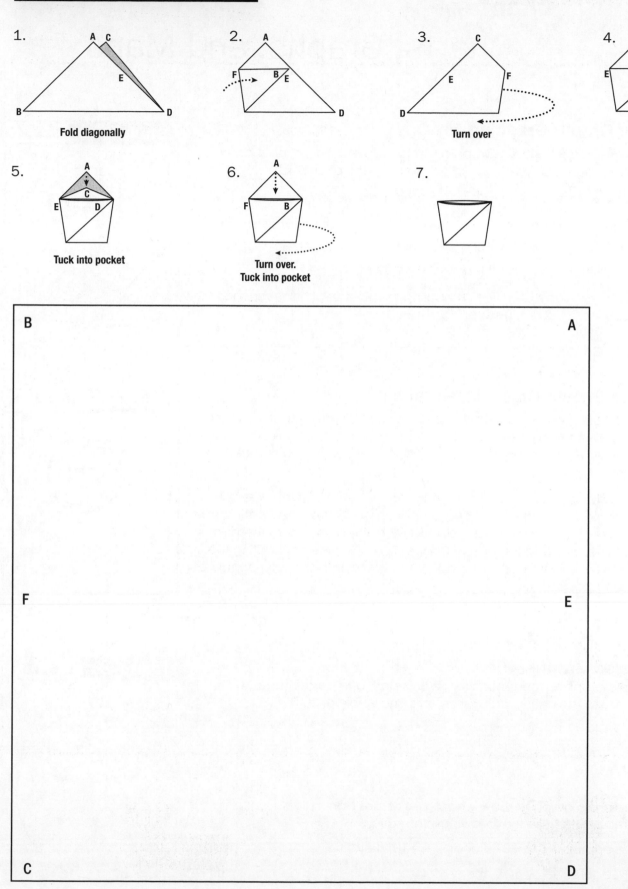

# Chapter 8
# Charts, Graphs, and Maps

## 1. Bar Graph: Graphing My Day

Standards 5, 8, 10

Use the graph on the Basic Graph page to create a bar graph showing how many hours a day you spend on the following activities:

● School   ● Homework   ● Sleeping   ● Eating Meals   ● Other Activities

copy page 87

Remember to label the horizontal axis and the vertical axis. Also, make sure you account for all 24 hours in the day!

Which activity do you spend the most time doing?_____

Write a comparison statement comparing the number of hours you spend in school to the number of hours you sleep.

_____

## 2. Line Graph: Class Attendance

Standards 5, 9, 10

Using the Basic Graph page, make a line graph to show the attendance for your class for one week. Along the horizontal axis, write the days of the school week. Along the vertical axis, starting with 1, write the number of students in your class.

copy page 87

Record daily attendance by finding the line for the day of the week on horizontal axis, and the line for the number on the vertical axis that represents the number of students in class that day. Mark the point where these lines intersect with a dot. At the end of the week, draw a line connecting the dots and describe what this line looks like. What does the line tell you about your class's attendance?

_____

## 3. Circle Graphs: Pies

Standards 1, 5, 10

In a circle graph, each section represents part, or a percentage, of the whole. The entire circle represents one whole or 100%.

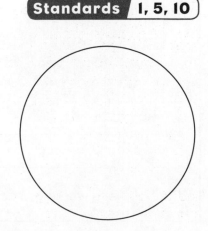

Fill in the circle graph to show what types of pies Darren likes to eat most often. Use the following information:

20% pumpkin    30% pecan    10% key lime

30% apple    10% cherry

## 4. Comparing Two Hobbies

Standards 5, 7

Look at the graph in Figure 2 on the Graph It page. What is the label on the horizontal axis (x-axis)?

_____

The vertical axis (y-axis)?

_____

Write one or two sentences describing what the graph shows about Ralph and Anya.

_____

_____

copy
page 88

## 5. Making a Graph to Compare Two Hobbies

Standards 5, 8, 10

Make a graph of your own like the one in Figure 2 on the Graph It page to represent the following information:

*Paula enjoys riding her bike but loves to swim.*

*Jan loves both swimming and riding her bike.*

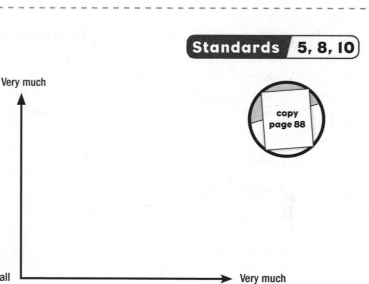

copy
page 88

## 6. Taking a Survey

Standards 5, 8, 9

You can conduct surveys to gather information about the likes and dislikes of people in your school. Decide what information you would like to gather, and write three questions to ask in your survey. You could ask about sports, hobbies, foods, music, and so on.

1. _____

2. _____

3. _____

Find 10 people to whom you can ask your survey questions. Graph your survey results.

What is your favorite ice cream flavor?

## 7. Using Coordinates to Plot Points on a Grid

Standards 3, 5

copy
page 89

Look at the grid in Figure 1 on the Grids and Charts page. The numbers across the bottom identify positions along the horizontal (x) axis. The letters along the left side identify positions on the vertical (y) axis. A number and a letter together can be used to identify the location of a point on the grid. The number and letter pair is called the *coordinates* of the point.

Draw a dot on the grid to show the point named by each of these coordinates:

| | | | |
|---|---|---|---|
| 9, E | 8, D | 8, F | 7, C |
| 7, G | 6, B | 6, H | 5, A |
| 5, I | 4, B | 4, H | 3, C |
| 3, G | 2, D | 2, F | 1, E |

Then connect the dots. What shape do you see?

## 8. Giving Directions to Draw Pictures on the Grid

Standards 3, 5, 7

2 copies
page 89

On one of the two copies of the Grids and Charts page, draw a simple picture, such as a heart, on the Figure 1 grid. Use straight lines that meet at coordinate points. Then, write the coordinates used to create your picture. Give a partner the coordinates of your drawing so he or she can copy it onto the other blank grid.

## 9. Categories

Standards 5, 9

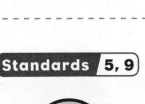

copy
page 89

Use Figure 2 on the Grids and Charts page. In the bottom spaces, write the letters *r, m, t,* and *p*. In the spaces along the left, write *food, animal, clothing, sport*. Move up and across to find out what to write in each square. For example, in the square where the *t* column intersects the *food* row, you must write a food that begins with *t*, such as *tacos* or *tomatoes*. Write one item in each square.

## 10. Always, Often, Sometimes, Never

Standards 5, 7, 9

Label the spaces along the bottom of the chart in Figure 2 on the Grids and Charts page *always, often, sometimes,* and *never*. Write the following activities along the left side of the chart: *do chores, study for tests, eat dessert, go to bed early*. Decide how often you do each of these activities and put a check in the appropriate box.

copy page 89

---

## 11. Using a Chart to Organize Information

Standards 5, 7, 8

Show how you could set up a chart to collect our data for these questions:

1. In which month do the greatest number of people in your class have their birthday?

2. Which recess game is the class favorite?

---

## 12. Making a Map

Standards 3, 5, 9, 10

Follow these directions to draw a map of a neighborhood:

a. Draw a grid with 3 horizontal lines and 3 vertical lines.

b. Label the horizontal lines from the bottom to the top *1st Street, 2nd Street,* and *3rd Street*.

c. Label the vertical lines from left to right *Hill Ave., Lake Ave.,* and *Park Ave.*

d. Write an *N* (for north) at the top of the map, an *S* (for south) on the bottom, a *W* (for west) on the left side, and an *E* (for east) on the right side.

e. Draw a triangle representing a school on the northeast corner of 3rd Street and Hill Ave.

f. Draw a square representing a park extending from Lake Ave. to Park Ave., and from 1st Street to 2nd Street.

g. Draw a circle representing a pond in the southwest corner of the park.

## 13. Finding Locations on a Map

Standards 3, 5, 8, 9, 10

Draw a place of interest on the map you made in Problem 12, such as a baseball field, outdoor skating rink, a mall, City Hall, and so on. On the other side of your map, write directions for traveling from the school to your new location using streets, avenues, and compass directions.

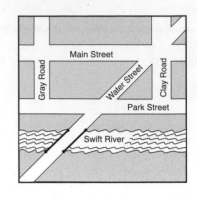

## 14. Creating a Map Legend

Standards 3, 5, 8

A map often has a **legend,** or key, that explains what the symbols used on it represent. Using the map you created in Problems 12 and 13, create a legend telling what each symbol represents.

**Bonus:** Create a map of your neighborhood that is similar to the map you created in Problem 12 and 13 and make a legend for it.

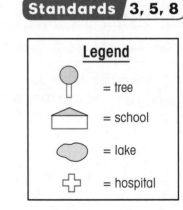

## 15. Using Scale on a Map

Standards 1, 4, 5, 6, 8

Maps are smaller than the areas they represent. A **scale** on a map tells how the measurements on the map compare with the actual measurements. For example, the scale on a map might be 1 inch equals 16 miles. If the distance between two towns on the map is 2 inches, the actual distance is 32 miles. What would be the actual distance if the distance on the map was ½ inch?

_____

Draw a large rectangle to use as the outline of a map. Use a scale of 1 centimeter equals 10 kilometers (1 cm = 10 km). You can think of a centimeter as being about equal to the width of your index finger. Label the towns of Riverville, Lakeville, Blueville, and Redville on your map using the following information:

a. Riverville is 50 km west of Lakeville.
b. Lakeville is 70 km north of Redville.
c. Blueville is about half the distance between Riverville and Redville.

1 in. = 16 mi.

1 cm. = 10 km.

## 16. Estimating to Compare Distances Between Towns on a Map

Standards 1, 4, 5

Look at the map on page 90. Estimate to compare distances between towns. Copy and complete this sentence in at least three different ways:

copy
page 90

1. _____ is about as far from _____

   as _____ is from _____.

2. _____ is about as far from _____

   as _____ is from _____.

3. _____ is about as far from _____

   as _____ is from _____.

## 17. Mapping the Classroom

Standards 1, 3, 4, 9

On a separate piece of paper, draw a map of your classroom! Make sure to include all important areas of the classroom and a legend for the map.

**Bonus:** Use a scale of 1 inch equals 1 foot. to estimate the number of feet across the room, between objects, and so on.

## 18. Designing a Dream Room

Standards 4, 5, 6, 8

Design the room of your dreams. Decide on a scale, such as 1 inch equals 1 foot or 1 centimeter equals 1 meter. Draw the objects in your room according to that scale. Color and label the furniture in your dream room.

Choose your scale:

 1 in. = 1 ft.

1 cm. = 1 m.

...giant, 2-level bed, basket ball hoop, ice cream freezer, climbing tree...

List the furniture you will use:

# Curriculum Connections

## Reading Speed (Reading)

Have students label three columns Book 1, Book 2, and Book 3 along the horizontal axis of the Basic Graph. Then tell them to label the vertical axis from 0 to 200 in intervals of 10. Time students as they read for 1 minute. Ask them to count the number of words they read (while still understanding the story) and record the result in the first column of their graphs. Have them exchange books and repeat the activity. Continue until students have recorded the number of words read in one minute for all three books. Encourage students to suggest a title for the graph.

Discuss factors that make a difference in reading speed, such as difficulty of material, number and size of pictures, size of print, number of words on a page, and so on.

## Hide the Marker (Sports and Recreation)

Have students play this game in groups of 2 to 4. Each player needs a copy of the grid in Figure 1, page 89, and some small marker, such as a centimeter cube. One player hides his or her marker on a point of the grid, keeping the grid out of view of the other players. The other players take turns naming coordinates, trying to guess where the marker is located. If the guess is not correct, the "hider" reveals one direction for the player to move (up, down, left, right) to go from the coordinate that was guessed to the hidden marker. The players move their own makers according to the clues the hider gives. The player who names the coordinates of the hidden marker hides it for the next game.

## Map Collections (Social Studies)

Collect a variety of maps, such as a road map of your city, highway maps of states, a political map of a country, a topographical map of a region, and so on. Display the maps for students to look at during free time. Ask them to compare two of the maps and write three ways the maps are alike and three ways they are different.

## Visit From an Architect (Social Studies)

Ask a parent or another adult who is an architect to visit your class and discuss his or her job, emphasizing how important math is to the profession.

# Basic Graph

|  |  |  |  |  |
|--|--|--|--|--|
|  |  |  |  |  |
|  |  |  |  |  |
|  |  |  |  |  |
|  |  |  |  |  |
|  |  |  |  |  |
|  |  |  |  |  |
|  |  |  |  |  |
|  |  |  |  |  |
|  |  |  |  |  |
|  |  |  |  |  |
|  |  |  |  |  |
|  |  |  |  |  |
|  |  |  |  |  |
|  |  |  |  |  |
|  |  |  |  |  |
|  |  |  |  |  |
|  |  |  |  |  |
|  |  |  |  |  |
|  |  |  |  |  |

# Graph It

Figure 1

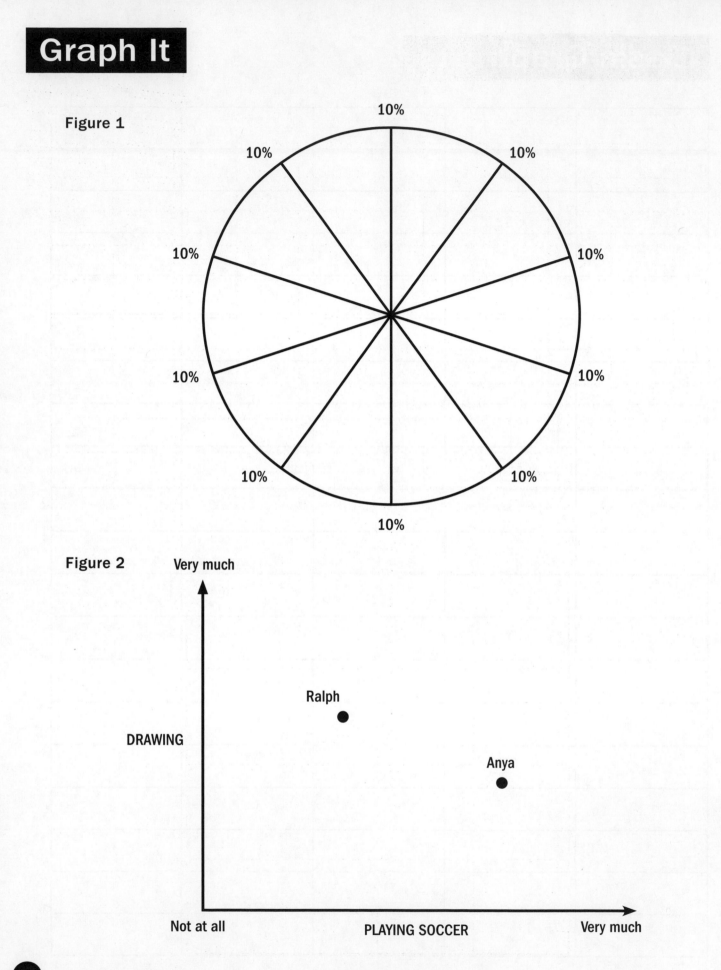

10%
10%
10%
10%
10%
10%
10%
10%
10%
10%

Figure 2

Very much

DRAWING

Ralph
●

Anya
●

Not at all          PLAYING SOCCER          Very much

# Grids and Charts

**Figure 1**

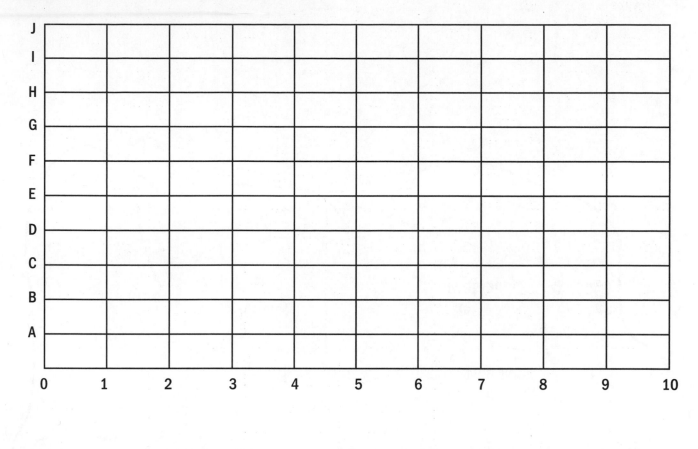

**Figure 2**

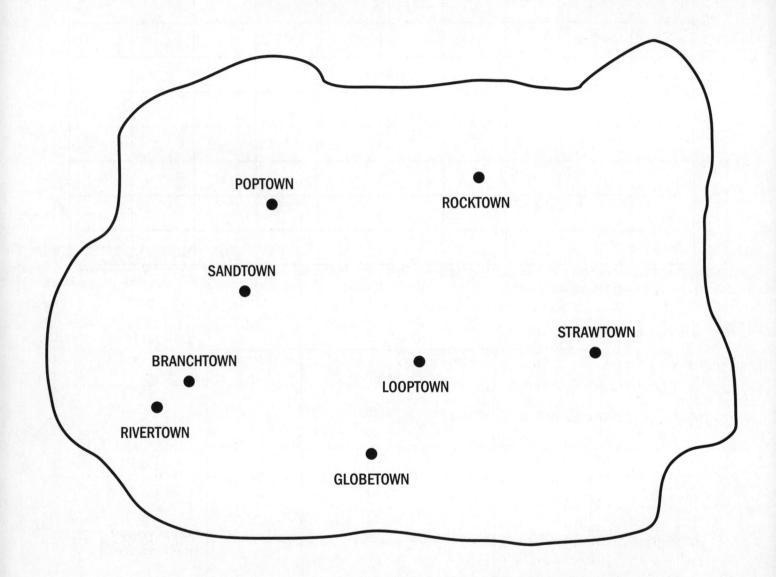

POPTOWN

ROCKTOWN

SANDTOWN

STRAWTOWN

BRANCHTOWN

LOOPTOWN

RIVERTOWN

GLOBETOWN

## Chapter 9
# Time and Money

## 1. Cycles in Nature and Measuring Time

Standards 4, 9

Long ago, people used cycles in nature to tell the passing of time and seasons. Match the element of nature with the unit of time to show how people told time.

- sun
- days and months

- moon
- months and years

- seasons
- hours and days

---

## 2. Days in a Year

Standards 1, 4, 9

Would the number of days in a year be greater or less than 365 if each month had 30 days?

_____

Why does a year last for 365 days?

_____

Predict why we have leap year every 4 years.

_____

_____

---

## 3. Time Measured in Twelfths

Standards 4, 9

The number 12 is a special number when it comes to measuring time. Name at least two ways we measure time in twelfths, or numbers that are divisible by 12.

1.

2.

What other numbers do we use to measure time?

## 4. Designing a Time Measurement System

Suppose you could change the way time is measured. Write a short story telling what changes you would make, and how the instruments we use to measure time, such as clocks and calendars, would be different.

_____

_____

_____

_____

_____

## 5. Days in a Month

Answer the following questions without looking at a calendar:

Draw a calendar to help you.

a. If the first day of the month is a Monday, what will be the dates of the other Mondays in the month?

_____, _____, _____, _____

b. If the first day of the month is Sunday, what will be the date of the first Saturday?

_____

## 6. Comparing Mars Years and Earth Years

It takes Mars 687 Earth days to orbit once around the sun. So, 1 year on Mars is 687 Earth days. About how many Earth years is 687 days?

Show your work.

_____

Estimate about how many days old you are. _____

How many years old would you be if Earth years were as long as Mars years?

_____

## 7. 24-Hour Clock

Standards 1, 4, 6, 7

In the military, people use a 24-hour clock. Look at the chart on the Military Time page. Midnight is 00 hours, 1 A.M. is 0100 hours, 2 A.M. is 0200 hours, and so on.

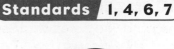

copy page 100

If Jan went to bed at 2100 and woke up at 0600, how many hours did she sleep?

_____

Write the time she went to bed on a 12-hour clock. _____

Now, write the time she woke up on a 12-hour clock. _____

***Bonus:*** When the hands on a military clock have gone around once, how many times have the hands on a 12-hour clock gone around?

## 8. Writing a Schedule Using Military Time

Standards 4, 9

Use the chart on the Military Time page to rewrite Mary's daily schedule using military time.

copy page 100

| MARY'S DAILY SCHEDULE | | |
|---|---|---|
| **Activity** | **12-hour Clock** | **Military Time** |
| Wake Up | 7:00 A.M. | |
| Go to School | 8:00 A.M. | |
| Lunch | 12:00 P.M. | |
| Practice Basketball | 3:00 P.M. | |
| Eat Dinner | 5:00 P.M. | |
| Homework | 7:00 P.M. | |
| Bedtime | 10:00 P.M. | |

***Bonus:*** Write your daily schedule using military time.

## 9. Inventions of the Past 200 Years

Standards 4, 6, 9

Tortoises live longer than any other animal. Some tortoises live to be 200 years old! Suppose you were born 200 years ago. List 5 things that have been invented or discovered during your lifetime—from 200 years ago to the present day.

1.

2.

3.

4.

5.

## 10. Birth Dates

Peg and Greg are twins. Peg was born at 11:57 P.M. on December 31, 1999. Greg was born 7 minutes later.

What time was Greg born? _____

What is Peg's birth date? _____

Greg's birth date? _____

---

## 11. Estimating Time

Lupe groaned as she looked at the clock after she, her mother, and her two sisters finished a spaghetti dinner. Her favorite TV show was starting, and it was her night to do the dishes! Lupe estimated it takes 10 seconds to wash each glass, 30 seconds to wash each dirty dish, and 1 minute to wash each dirty pan or serving bowl. She can wash all the silverware in 5 minutes. She needs to wash the following dishes:

1 spaghetti pot
1 tomato sauce pot
1 salad bowl
1 fork, 1 knife, and 1 spoon per person
1glass, 1 salad plate, 1 dinner plate, and 1 dessert bowl per person

About how many minutes of her favorite program will Lupe miss? _____

---

## 12. Work Shifts

Use the Venn diagram below to show whether people in the following jobs work during the daytime hours, the nighttime hours, or both:

a cook, a teacher, a police officer, a secretary, a security guard, a bank teller, a grocery clerk, a doctor, a firefighter, a mail carrier.

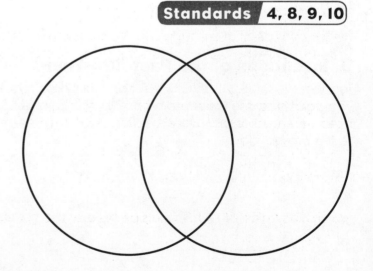

## 13. Making a Game Schedule

**Standards**  I, 4, 6, 9

The Little Sluggers baseball games last 1 hour and 30 minutes. The coaches need to schedule 5 games on the same baseball field on a Saturday. All teams must be off the field by 5:00. Complete the schedule to show when each of the 5 games can be played if you allow 15 minutes in between games.

| Game | Time |
|------|------|
| Game 1 | |
| Game 2 | |
| Game 3 | |
| Game 4 | |
| Game 5 | |

## 14. Making an After-School Schedule

**Standards**  I, 4, 6, 9

Every Friday, Sonja's class has a test. The teacher asks students to study about 2 hours during the week for the test. Sonja likes to play outside in the afternoons, and her bedtime is 8:30. Sonja also reads for 30 minutes every night.

Complete the after-school schedule for Sonja that includes her study time, the other activities mentioned, and other things Sonja might do in the evenings.

| Time | Activity |
|------|----------|
| | |
| | |
| | |
| | |
| 8:30 | go to bed |

## 15. Objects Used as Money

**Standards**  I, 4, 9

Money has been in use for a very, very long time. People used shells, stones, clay, and other objects for money before it was made from metal and paper.

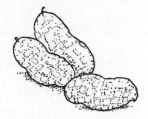

Suppose peanuts were used for money. If 3 peanuts are equal in value to a penny, how many peanuts equal

A nickel? _____     A dime? _____

A quarter? _____     A dollar? _____

Would the value of 100 peanuts be greater than or less than 40¢?

_____

## 16. Creating a Money System

Standards 1, 4, 6, 7, 10

Invent a money system using objects from nature in place of coins or dollar bills. For example, 5 pebbles might equal 1 shell—or it might cost 2 shells to buy 1 soda. Write or draw a description of your money system showing how many of 1 object it takes to equal the value of another object.

Using your money system, show the price of three things, such as an ice cream cone, a movie, or a pair of jeans.

Prices of common items:

1. _____  _____

2. _____  _____

3. _____  _____

| NEW MONEY SYSTEM ||
| Object | Value |
| --- | --- |
|  |  |
|  |  |
|  |  |
|  |  |
|  |  |
|  |  |

## 17. Identifying Coins

Standards 4, 9

Use the first row of cards on the Coin Cards page. Look at the president pictured on each coin. Arrange the coins in the order described by these clues:

a. The two most famous presidents are facing each other.
   **Hint!** They appear on the highest and lowest value coins.

b. The president with a beard is first.

c. The two presidents with pony tails are next to each other.

d. The most recent president is last.
   **Hint!** He is on the coin with the second highest value.

copy
page 101

Write the coins in order. What is the value of the four coins together?

_____  _____  _____  _____ = _____
     coin 1            coin 2            coin 3            coin 4            total value

## 18. Matching Coins and Amounts

Standards 1, 4, 10

Use the Coin Cards page to help you find a combination of coins that equals each amount given. Record the name and number of coins shown on each card.

copy
page 101

a. Find 3 coins that can be combined to equal 40¢. _____

b. Find 11 coins that can be combined to equal 15¢. _____

c. Find 4 coins that can be combined to equal 12¢. _____

d. Find 4 coins that can be combined to equal 50¢. _____

e. Find 5 coins that can be combined to equal 18¢. _____

## 19. Different Ways to Show 25¢

Standards  1, 4, 6, 10

Look at the Coin Cards page and record 10 different ways you can show 25¢ using the cards.

copy page 101

1. _____    6. _____

2. _____    7. _____

3. _____    8. _____

4. _____    9. _____

5. _____    10. _____

## 20. Decision Making

Standards  4, 6, 7, 9

Raul and Ariel are going to spend 2 hours at an amusement park. The park has food booths, game booths, and rides. They each have $10 to spend. They each have a choice of paying 75¢ for each ride, or paying $10.00 for an unlimited number of rides. What do Raul and Ariel need to think about in order to make their decision?

 Make a list.

- 
- 
- 
- 

## 21. Determining Savings Using a Calendar

Standards  1, 4, 6, 9

 Show your work.

Charlene wants to save her money for a CD that costs $15.00. She gets a $3.00 allowance every Monday. Charlene also has a job walking the neighbor's dog once a day. Each time she walks the dog, she receives $1.00. If Charlene saves all of her money each week, how long will it take her to save enough money to buy the CD?

_____

How long would it take her to save enough money to buy 2 CDs at the same price?

_____

## 22. Making a Purchase

Standards 1, 4

copy page 102

Look at what is for sale in the shop windows of the Mini Mall. Suppose you won a $50.00 gift certificate.

a. Write 2 different ways you could spend all or some of the $50 at the Mini Mall. Include the items you would buy as well as how much each way would cost.

1.                                    2.

b. How much more money would you need to buy a pair of in-line skates?

_____         A dollhouse kit? _____

## 23. Comparing Regular Prices and Sale Prices

Standards 1, 7, 10

copy page 102

The Mini Mall shops are advertising sales. Create a table to compare the regular prices with the sale prices. Use the following information:

a. Each CD is regularly priced at $12.99.

b. Everything in the sporting goods store is half the regular price.

c. Dollhouses usually sell for $89.98, and dolls are $10.00 each.

d. Paperback books are normally $4.85.

| Item | Sale Price | Regular Price |
|------|-----------|---------------|
|      |           |               |
|      |           |               |
|      |           |               |
|      |           |               |
|      |           |               |
|      |           |               |

## 24. Making Change

Standards 1, 4, 8

Suppose you are a cashier. Tell what change you would give. Use mental math when you can. Someone gives you:

a. $1 for a 15¢ item. _____

c. $10 for 2 items that cost $5.60 and $4.40. _____

b. $5 for something that costs $3.99. _____

d. $20 for 3 items that cost $6.25 each. _____

# Curriculum Connections

## Make a Sundial (Science)

Follow these directions to make a sundial. You may wish to have small groups make a sundial or make 1 sundial together as a class.

> a. Place a dowel in the ground where there is sunlight all day long.

b. Draw a circle around the dowel.

c. Mark and label the places on the circle the shadow points toward at 9:00 A.M., 10:00 A.M., 11:00 A.M., 12:00 noon, 1:00 P.M., 2:00 P.M., and so on.

Check the sundial against a clock or watch daily, making adjustments until it is accurate.

Ask questions about the experience, such as, *When does the shadow increase in length? Decrease in length? Is there a time when the shadow nearly disappears?*

## World Records (Social Studies)

Provide students with the following information: A group of college students claim to have made the longest phone call in the world—they talked for over 720 hours.

Have students determine how many days 720 hours equal. Ask students to work in small groups using a world's record book, or books, to research three other unusual things people have done for a record amount of time. Make a class chart showing the record time for each event.

## Money Around the World (Social Studies)

Tell students to find out what money is called in other countries, and compare its value to the U.S. dollar. (The foreign money exchange rates can be found on the financial pages of most newspapers.) If possible, bring in, or have students bring in, currency from other countries. Display the money and discuss similarities and differences.

# Military Time

| 24-Hour Clock Time | Military Time | 24-Hour Clock Time | Military Time |
| --- | --- | --- | --- |
| 12 midnight | = 00 hours | 12 noon | = 1200 hours |
| 12:30 A.M. | = 0030 hours | 12:30 P.M. | = 1230 hours |
| 1 A.M. | = 0100 hours | 1 P.M. | = 1300 hours |
| 2 A.M. | = 0200 hours | 2 P.M. | = 1400 hours |
| 3 A.M. | = 0300 hours | 3 P.M. | = 1500 hours |
| 4 A.M. | = 0400 hours | 4 P.M. | = 1600 hours |
| 5 A.M. | = 0500 hours | 5 P.M. | = 1700 hours |
| 6 A.M. | = 0600 hours | 6 P.M. | = 1800 hours |
| 7 A.M. | = 0700 hours | 7 P.M. | = 1900 hours |
| 8 A.M. | = 0800 hours | 8 P.M. | = 2000 hours |
| 9 A.M. | = 0900 hours | 9 P.M. | = 2100 hours |
| 10 A.M. | = 1000 hours | 10 P.M. | = 2200 hours |
| 11 A.M. | = 1100 hours | 11 P.M. | = 2300 hours |

*Daily Math Jumpstarts* • Scholastic

# Coin Cards

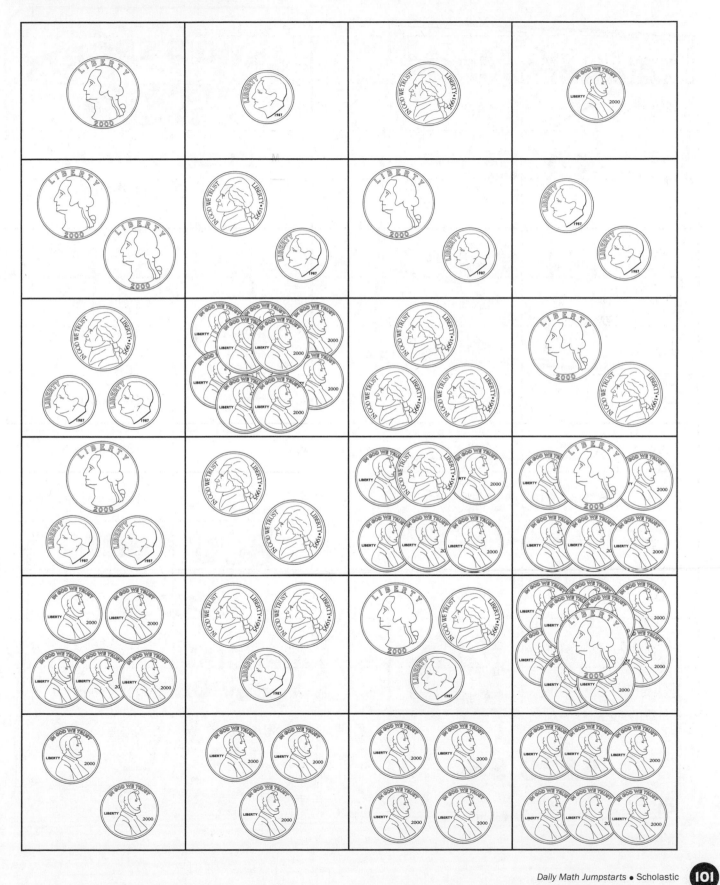

# Miguel's Music

**SALE!**

2 CD's for only

**$21.00**

# SPUD'S SPORTS

**SALE!**

**EVERYTHING IN THE STORE IS HALF OFF!**

| | |
|---|---|
| Running Shoes: | Now $25.75 |
| In-Line Skates: | Just $59.95 |
| Helmets: | Only $19.95 |

# DELIA'S DOLLHOUSES

**HURRY SALE!**

Just in...complete dollhouse kit!

Includes 4 dolls!

Won't Last!!

**$129.98**

# Best Ever Books

**SPECIAL Today Only!**

3 paperbacks for

**$12.00**

# Chapter 10
# Measurement

## 1. Nonstandard Units of Measure

Standards 4, 6, 8

Long ago, people measured length using the length of their own feet as the unit of measure. Since people have different sizes of feet, this caused some problems. What problems could have occurred because people used their feet to measure?

_____

How do you think they solved the problem?

_____

## 2. Unusual Units of Measure

Standards 4, 8, 9

Some unusual units are used for measuring very specific things. For example, the height of horses is measured in hands. One hand equals 4 inches. The speed of a boat is measured in knots. One knot equals 6,076 feet.

Make up your own unit of measurement for distance, volume, speed, or length.

| New unit of measure | Type (distance, volume, speed, length) | Standard unit equivalent | What you'd use it to measure |
|---|---|---|---|
|  |  |  |  |

## 3. Accurate Measures

Standards 4, 9

Make a list of four situations for which it is very important to have accurate measurements. Explain why accurate measurements are important for each situation.

1.

2.

3.

4.

## 4. Estimation: Comparing Measures

Standards 1, 4

Use the Comparison Cards page to make estimates about objects in your classroom.

copy
page 112

---

## 5. Reference Measures

Standard 4

You may not know it, but your hand is a convenient ruler! For most people, the width of the index fingertip is about 1 centimeter. And most people have one finger in which the distance from the top knuckle to the fingertip is 1 inch. Use a ruler to find out for which of your fingers this is true.

Use your "built-in ruler" to find the length of your pencil and two other things at your desk. Record the answers both in inches and centimeters, and then check your answers using a real ruler.

| Object | Estimated length (in) | Estimated length (cm) | Actual length (in) | Actual length (cm) |
|---|---|---|---|---|
|  |  |  |  |  |
|  |  |  |  |  |
|  |  |  |  |  |

---

## 6. Estimating Length

Standards 1, 4

Estimate how many pennies placed in a row it would take to measure 1 foot. Check your estimate.

Estimated number of pennies in 1 foot _____

Actual number of pennies _____

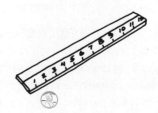

## 7. Inch, Foot, Yard

If 12 inches equal 1 foot, and 3 feet equal 1 yard, then how many inches equal 1 yard?

_____

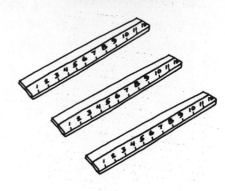

Find three things in the classroom that each measure about 1 yard.

1.

2.

3.

---

## 8. Using Inches, Feet, and Yards

Write two things that you would measure using inches, two things you would measure using feet, and two things you would measure using yards.

Inches: 1. _____   2. _____

Feet:   1. _____   2. _____

Yards:  1. _____   2. _____

---

## 9. Making and Adjusting Estimates of Length

Suppose 10 students stood next to each other and held hands, stretching their arms as far as possible. Estimate how long the line they make would measure.

_____

Did you know that if you stretch out your arms and measure the distance from fingertip to fingertip, the measurement will be the same as your actual height? Use this information to make a new estimate of the total length of the outstretched arms of 10 students.

_____

Which do you think is the better estimate, your first estimate or your second estimate? Explain.

_____

## 10. If You Were 30 Inches Tall

Standards 4, 7, 9

Suppose you were 30 inches tall.

a. List three things in the room that would be taller than you.

1. _____

2. _____

3. _____

b. Name two things you often do at school that would be difficult or impossible to do.

1. _____

2. _____

c. Name two things that you could do at 30 inches tall that would be difficult or impossible to do if you were your normal height.

1. _____

2. _____

## 11. Estimating Length

Standards 4, 9

Estimate in centimeters:

1. the length of your foot _____

2. the length of each of your fingers and thumb on 1 hand

_____   _____   _____   _____   _____

Is the estimated total of your fingers and thumb greater than or less than the estimate of your foot?

_____

Measure to the nearest centimeter to check your estimates.

## 12. Identifying an Object by Length

Standards 4, 7

Use the pictures on the Measuring Objects page to find the mystery object described below:

The mystery object is longer than 10 cm. It is not the longest object, but it has the greatest perimeter. What is it?

_____

copy
page 113

## 13. Describing Objects Using Measurements

**Standards** 4, 7, 8

Using the objects on the Measuring Objects page , make up your own measurement mystery giving two clues.

1. _____

2. _____

copy page 113

---

## 14. Perimeter

**Standards** 3, 4, 10

Cut out the squares in Figure 1 on the Measuring Squares page. Each square is 1 inch long and 1 inch wide. Make a figure with 8 squares. (Make sure that any 2 squares placed next to each other touch along the entire side.)

Measure the distance around the figure you made by counting the outside edges of the squares. The distance around a figure is called the **perimeter**.

_____

If you make a different figure using the 8 squares, would the perimeter change?

_____

Use the 8 squares to make a figure with the greatest perimeter you can and one with the least perimeter. Record the perimeter.

greatest: _____    least: _____

copy page 114

Show your work.

---

## 15. Area

**Standards** 3, 4, 10

When you find how much space a figure covers you are finding the area of the figure. It is measured in square units. Use all 25 of the 1-inch squares in Figure 1 of the Measuring Square page to make three separate figures. What is the area of each figure?

On a separate piece of paper, trace around the outside of your figures, record each area, and color them.

Area measurements:

Shape 1 _____

Shape 2 _____

Shape 3 _____

copy page 114

## 16. Area and Perimeter

Standards 2, 3, 4, 10

Make six different figures using the square inches in Figure 1 on the Measuring Squares page. Record the perimeter and area of the figures you make in the chart in Figure 2 on the same page.

copy
page 114

## 17. Comparing Areas and Perimeters

copy
page 115

Standards 4, 9

Look at the shapes on the Area and Perimeter page. Use the grid (each square is 1 square centimeter) at the top of the page to help measure each shape's area and perimeter. Record your measurements below.

Which figures have the same area?

_____

The same perimeter?

_____

| Figure | Area (sq cm) | Perimeter (cm) |
|--------|--------------|----------------|
| A      |              |                |
| B      |              |                |
| C      |              |                |
| D      |              |                |
| E      |              |                |
| F      |              |                |

## 18. Measuring Sound

Standards 4, 9

Sounds we hear are measured in **decibels**. The softest sound humans can hear is about 0 decibels. A normal speaking tone is about 60 decibels. Humans find it very uncomfortable to listen to a sound measuring 130 decibels.

Think of four different sounds you often hear. Write your four sounds on the scale where you think they belong.

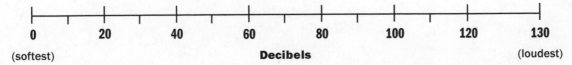

| 0 | 20 | 40 | 60 | 80 | 100 | 120 | 130 |

(softest)                    Decibels                    (loudest)

## 19. Equivalent Measures

Standards 1, 4, 9

Use the following information to complete the table at right.

16 tablespoons = 1 cup

1 gallon = 4 quarts

1 quart = 4 cups

1 pint = 2 cups

| TABLE OF MEASURES | |
|---|---|
| **Unit of Measure** | **Number of Ounces** |
| 1 tablespoon | |
| 1 cup | 8 |
| 1 pint | |
| 1 quart | |
| 1 gallon | |

## 20. Temperature

Standards 4, 8, 9

If you are looking at a Fahrenheit thermometer, tell whether the following temperatures feel cold, cool, warm, or hot.

45° F _____

60° F _____

75° F _____

90° F _____

30° F _____

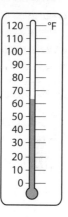

## 21. Below-Zero Temperatures

Standard 4

On a very cold winter morning, a Fahrenheit thermometer showed that the temperature was 6 degrees below zero. In the early afternoon, the thermometer showed that the temperature was 25 degrees. How many degrees did the temperature rise?

 Show your work.

## 22. Weight Versus Volume

Predict how cereal in a cereal box is measured.

_____

_____

Why does a box of cereal sometimes not feel very full compared to another box the same size?

_____

_____

---

## 23. Comparing Size

Close your eyes and picture a jar filled with small marbles. Now picture a jar the same size filled with large marbles. Open your eyes and draw a picture of what you saw. Which jar do you think holds more marbles?

_____

Explain why you think this.

_____

_____

| Jar with small marbles | Jar with large marbles |
|---|---|
|  |  |

---

## 24. Measuring Weight

At a grocery store, a sign says that apples are 99¢ a pound. If you don't have a scale, how could you tell whether 4 apples are less than, greater than, or equal to 1 pound?

_____

_____

_____

# Curriculum Connections

## Measure Treasure Hunt (Physical Education)

Divide the class into small groups. Ask each group to find two things that:

   a. weigh less than a textbook.

   b. are thicker than a piece of chalk.

   c. can hold more liquid than a coffee mug.

## Go the Distance (Sports and Recreation)

Make a 10-foot measuring rope by tying a knot at one end of a clothesline. Tie additional knots at 1-foot intervals, so that there are 11 knots in all. Cut off any extra clothesline at each end. Students can count the knots to measure how far they can broad-jump or travel in three hops.

## Metric Debate (Social Studies)

Nearly every country in the world except the United States uses the metric system of measurement exclusively. American scientists use the metric system, and so do Olympic athletes.

   Discuss the advantages of countries using the same measurement system. Elicit that metric measure equivalencies are based on multiples of 10—10 millimeters equal 1 centimeter, 100 centimeters equal 1 meter, and so on. Have students compare that to customary measure equivalencies. Ask them which system of equivalencies they think is easier to remember.

   Brainstorm a list of things that would need to change if the United States were to use the metric system exclusively. Some examples are mileage signs on roadways, weight information on food packages, reporting of rainfall and snowfall, and so on.

## Supermarket Survey (Nutrition/ Science)

Have students bring in lists of five or six food items and the units used to measure them. For example, soda may be measured in ounces or liters; milk is measured in pints, quarts, and gallons; sugar is often measured in pounds.

# Comparison Cards

1. _____

is as tall

as_____.

4. _____

is wider

than _____.

2. _____

is shorter

than _____.

5. _____

is the same width

as_____.

3. _____ and _____

are the same distance apart

as _____ and _____.

6. _____

holds as much

as_____.

# Measuring Objects

| centimeters | | | | |
|---|---|---|---|---|
| 0 | 5 | 10 | 15 | 20 |

**pencil** (18 cm x 1 cm)

**candy bar** (14 cm x 6 cm)

**calculator** (12 cm x 9 cm)

**chalk** (8 cm x 2 cm)

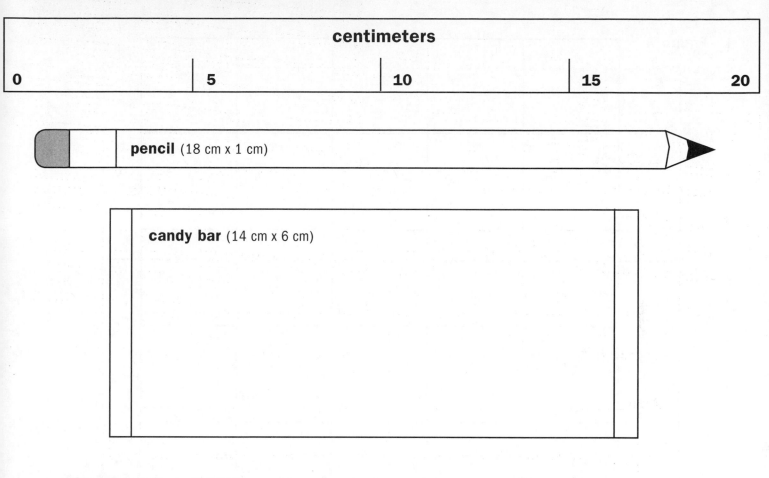
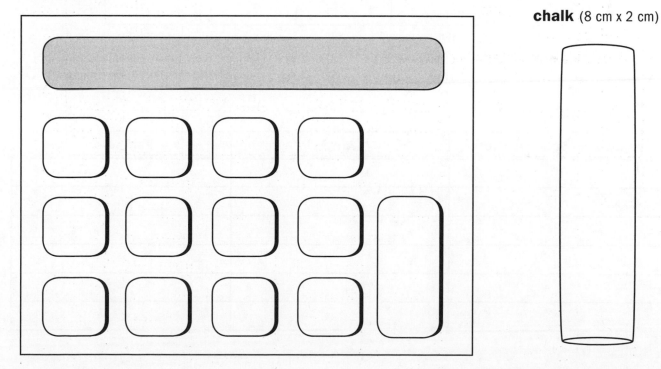

# Measuring Squares

Figure 1

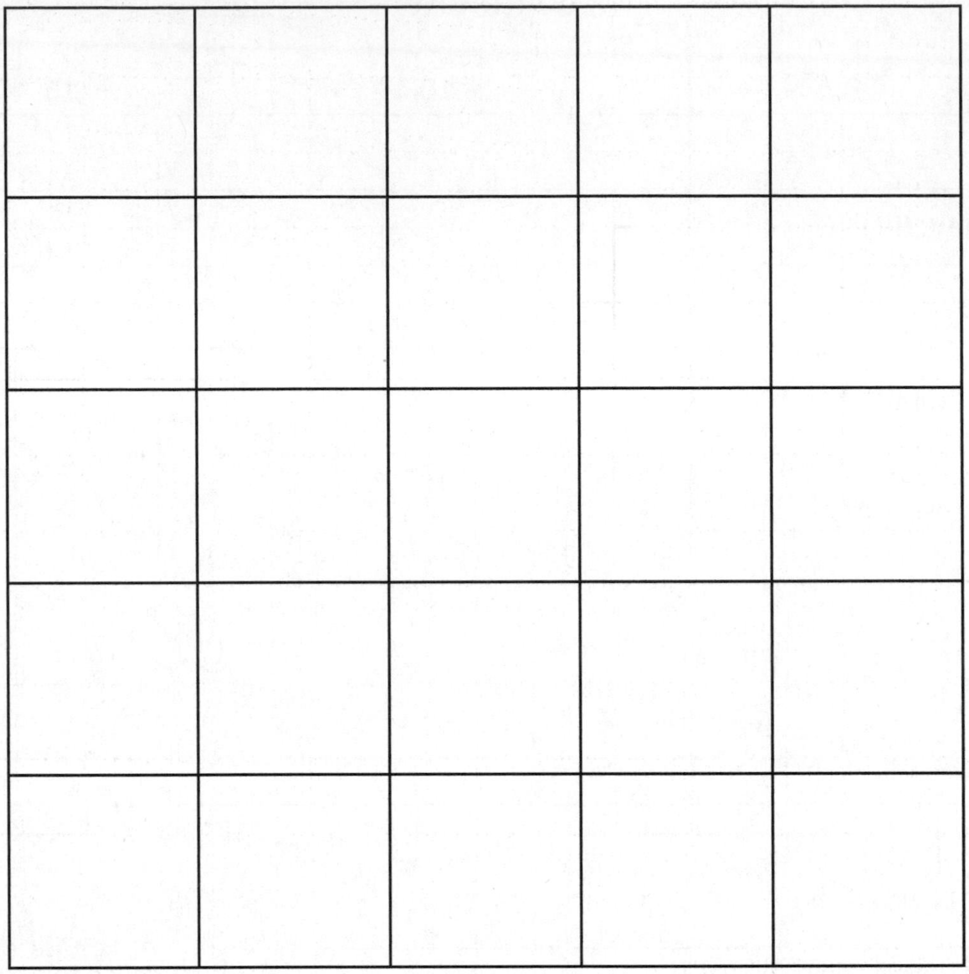

Figure 2

| Number of Squares Used | Area | Perimeter |
|---|---|---|
| | | |
| | | |
| | | |
| | | |
| | | |
| | | |

# Area and Perimeter

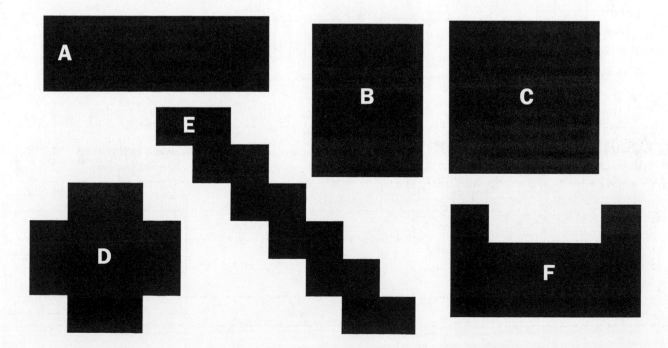

## Chapter 11
# Problem Solving

## 1. Solving a Number Puzzle

Complete the circle puzzle on the Number Puzzles page following these directions: Write a number in each of the empty sections. The numbers must be placed so that each number is opposite a number that is double its value or half its value. The sum of all the numbers in the puzzle should be 36.

**Standards** 1, 6

copy
page 121

## 2. Magic Square

In a magic square, numbers are placed so that each column, row, and diagonal has the same sum. On the Number Puzzles page complete the magic square so that there is a number from 1 to 9 in each box. Each number can be used only once. The sum of each column, row, and diagonal should be 15.

**Standards** 1, 6

copy
page 121

## 3. Creating a Magic Square

Create your own magic square, writing the numbers from 1 to 9 in different boxes in the square. Remember, each number can be used only once. Explain how you decided where to place the numbers.

**Standards** 1, 6, 7

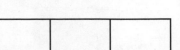

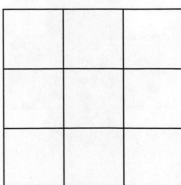

## 4. Finding All Possible Combinations

**Standards** 2, 5, 6

Show your work.

Marcus, Alex, and Victor went on a picnic. They each brought 2 different foods. Altogether they had peanut butter sandwiches and cheese sandwiches, bananas and apples, bags of corn chips and bags of potato chips. How many different lunches could they make if they took 1 sandwich, 1 piece of fruit, and 1 bag of chips for each lunch?

_____

## 5. Logical Thinking

**Standards** 6, 7, 8

A boy and a girl are sitting next to each other. One of them has red hair and the other one has black hair. The one with black hair says, "I am a boy." The one with red hair says, "I am a girl." At least one of them is not telling the truth. Which one is the boy and which one is the girl? Explain your answer.

## 6. Odd and Even Numbers

**Standards** 1, 2, 6

Show your work.

If the year you were born is an even-numbered year, and this year is an even-numbered year, will your age on your birthday this year be an odd or an even number?

_____

What if the year you were born was odd and this year is odd, is your age odd or even?

_____

Will your age be an odd or even number if the year you were born is an odd number, and this year is an even number?

_____

Write a rule you can use to tell for any year whether your age on your birthday that year will be an even or odd number.

_____

## 7. Measuring Precipitation

Standards 1, 6, 9

**Precipitation** is the amount of water that falls on the earth. It takes about 10 inches of snow to equal the same amount of water as 1 inch of rain.

If an area of land receives 30 inches of precipitation in a year, what are 5 different combinations of snow and rain it could have received?

|   | Inches of snow | Inches of rain |
|---|----------------|----------------|
| 1 |                |                |
| 2 |                |                |
| 3 |                |                |
| 4 |                |                |
| 5 |                |                |

## 8. Calculating Time

Standards 1, 4, 6, 7

At a water park, it takes 4 minutes to climb to the top of the water slide, and 1 minute to slide down it. Once they've landed in the pool below, people usually spend between 30 seconds and 2 minutes splashing around before getting out.

What is the greatest number of trips up and down the slide someone could make in 30 minutes?

_____

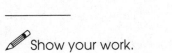Show your work.

## 9. Fact Families

Standards 1, 6

Number fact families are made up of two or three numbers that together make at least two related number sentences. For example, 4, 25, and 100 are a fact family. The numbers can be used to make the following sentences: 25 x 4 = 100; 4 x 25 = 100; 100 ÷ 4 = 25; and 100 ÷ 25 = 4.

Write number sentences for the following fact families:

a. 7, 56, 8 _____, _____, _____, _____

b. 54, 6, 9 _____, _____, _____, _____

c. 17, 8, 9 _____, _____, _____, _____

## 10. Adding Fractions

Standards 1, 4, 6, 10

copy page 122

Look at the Letter Ruler. Each quarter of an inch is labeled with a letter of the alphabet. To find the value of a word, find where each letter of the word is located on the ruler and add the measures together. For example, the letter *A* is located at ¼ inch; the letter *T* at 5 inches. So, the value of the word *at* equals ¼ + 5, or 5¼ inches.

What is the value of your first name? What is the value of the statement *math is fun*? Give the value and write a number sentence for each.

Your name _____  _____

Math is fun _____  _____

Which has a greater value? _____

---

## 11. Probability

Standards 5, 6, 7

It was dark in the morning when Jesse was getting dressed. He reached into his sock drawer, where he kept 10 pairs of white socks and 5 pairs of black socks. (Of course, they weren't together in pairs!) What is the least number of socks Jesse would need to pull out of his drawer before he could be positive he'd have two matching socks?

_____

Explain your answer.

_____

_____

---

## 12. Probability With Number Cards

Standards 2, 6, 7

Magda and Bruce were playing with a set of cards numbered 1 to 24. "I'll bet I can pull a number greater than 20 out of this set of cards," said Magda. "I have a better chance of pulling out an even number than you do of pulling out a number greater than 20," claimed Bruce. Who was right?

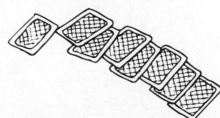

_____

Explain.

_____

_____

_____

# Curriculum Connections

## Logical Scenes (Language Arts)

Read aloud the following problem about the cat, the mouse, and the cheese and have students act out the solution.

A man had to take a cat, a mouse, and some cheese across a river in a boat. His boat was so small, though, he could only take one of them across at a time. He couldn't leave the cat alone with the mouse, or the mouse alone with the cheese. How could the man get all three across the river safely? How many trips across the river will it take?

## Making and Testing Predictions (Language Arts)

Predict which vowel is used most often in the English language. To check your prediction, count 100 words from one or more pages in a book. Work with a partner to make a tally of the number of times each vowel occurs in those 100 words. Which vowel occurs most often?

Repeat the activity for another set of 100 words. Does your answer change? How did your answer compare to your prediction?

## World Shopping Trip (Social Studies)

Tell students to suppose they can visit anywhere in the world they would like, and they have $3000.00 to spend. They must use the money to buy a plane ticket, plus cover the cost of lodging and meals for a week. Students can research the cost of the trip and make up an expense log for it. In the log, they should record how much their lodging costs each night, the price of the plane ticket, and the cost of each meal.

## Designing a 1-Minute Workout (Sports and Recreation)

Sometimes we feel as though we've been sitting still too long, and we need to exercise our muscles. Have students work with a partner to create a 1-minute exercise workout. The workout plan must include at least three different exercises. Students should estimate how many times they think each exercise can be done. Tell pairs to take turns timing and performing the exercise routine until they get the timing down to 1 minute.

# Number Puzzles

**Circle Puzzle**

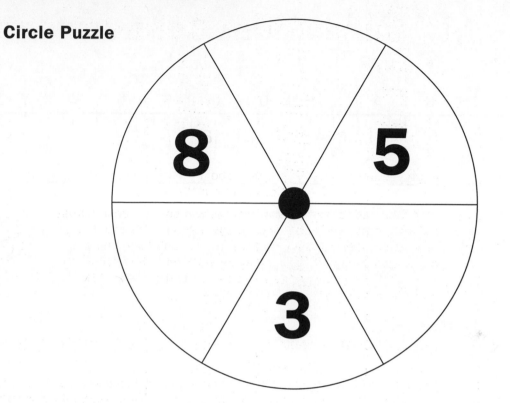

**Magic Square**

| | 1 | |
|---|---|---|
| 7 | | |
| | | 4 |

# Letter Ruler

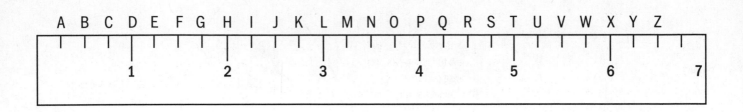

# Answer Key

## Chapter 1

### Page 7

1. Answers will vary, but may include: divide slices equally among friends, use ratios to compare the number of pieces of one type of topping with that of another, use fractions to show how many pieces you ate, figure out the price of one slice.

2. Answers will vary, but may include: timing races, calculating speed, comparing scores, calculating scores.

3. Answers will vary, but may include: words relating to temperature (*degrees Fahrenheit, degrees Celsius*), time of weather changes or duration of storms (*hours, overnight*), wind speeds (*miles per hour*), predicted or actual measures of rain or snow (*inches, feet*), probability (*percent, chance*).

### Page 8

4. Answers will vary. Sports may include: basketball, football, volleyball, baseball, soccer.

5. Answers will vary, but may include: a. 8 hours, b. 8 hours, c. 2 inches.

6. Change *cents* to *dollars, feet* to *miles, year* to *minute*.

### Page 9

7. Accept reasonable answers. Trotting and jogging are generally faster than striding and marching, which in turn, are faster than sauntering or tiptoeing. One possible response: Tania, Jaime, Sarah, Marcus, Sally, Toshio.

8. Lists will vary, but may include: get dressed, eat, wash, and collect homework. Times will vary, but the time it takes Jasmine to do everything on the list, when added to the time she needs to get up, should bring the time to 8:00.

9. Questions will vary, but may include: *How much did the two hats cost altogether?* or, *How much more did Amber pay for her hat than her sister?*

### Page 10

10. Accept reasonable responses. One possible response: She needs to know the length and height of the section of the fence that needs to be repaired, how much each foot of fencing costs, and how much it will cost to pay somebody to put in the new fencing if she cannot do it herself.

11. Lists will vary. Situations that might take about the same amount of time include: waiting your turn in a game and waiting in line for a drink of water; waiting for the bus and waiting for food in a restaurant (dependent, of course on the timeliness of the bus and the type of restaurant); sample list: 1. fountain, 2. game, 3. bus, 4. food, 5. birthday or special holiday.

12. All the words mean "three of something." Words for "two" will vary, but may include: pair, bicycle, biathlon, double play, double dip, twins. Check students' drawings.

### Page 11

13. Answers will vary. One possible answer: Find out the regular price of each pair of jeans. Divide the price of jeans that is ¼ off by 4, then subtract that amount from the regular price. Divide the price of jeans that is ⅓ off by 3, then subtract that amount from the regular price. Compare the two sale prices.

14. Lists will vary. Ways Willy can keep track may include: He can look at the store receipt, identify the coupon deductions, and find the sum of all the deductions.

15. Prices will vary, but may include: jeans—$20, sneakers—$40, T-shirt—$10. Check students' word problems.

### Page 12

16. about 4 months; answers will vary; lists will vary according to the season(s).

17. Answers and drawings will vary, but may include: eggs, flowers, doughnuts, cookies.

18. Answers and/or drawings will vary, but may include: a set of 26 alphabet cards; problems will vary, but may include: Sam has a set of 26 alphabet cards. If he removes all the letters that are vowels, how many cards are left in the set?

### Page 13

19. Venn diagrams will vary.

20. Venn diagrams will vary. Accept reasonable responses.

21. Check students' Venn diagrams.

### Page 14

22. oatmeal cookies

23. Answers will vary; possible responses include: the number of students who usually eat the school lunch, the school's attendance figures, and so on.

24. Estimates will vary; number of words on pages will vary. Either estimate may be closer to the actual number, but it is more likely that the second estimate will be closer since it's based on more information.

## Chapter 2

### Page 17

1. 3 + 3 + 3, or 9, animals; check student's drawings.

2. Totals will vary; color point systems will vary. New totals can be greater, less, or the same as the first totals.

3. Totals will vary; last names will usually have the greatest number of points because they may contain the most letters.

### Page 18

4. Illustrations and story problems will vary. Addition problems can be 7 + 7, 6 + 8, 9 + 5, 10 + 4, 11 + 3, 12 + 2, 13 +1, or 14 + 0.

5. 0 + 100, 1 + 99, 2 + 98, 3 + 97, . . . 50 + 50. Strategies will vary. Possible strategies include: To begin with combinations of numbers ending in 0, such as 10 + 90; finding a pattern such as 100 + 0, 99 + 1, 98 + 2, and so on; thinking of dollars and cents: 25 + 75, 50 + 50.

6. Number sentences will vary but may include 50 + 0, 49 +1, 48 + 2, 47 + 3, and so on. Students should realize that there are many more addition sentences that can be written for the number 100 than for 50.

## Page 19

7. Order of expressions may vary, but each row should include some of the following:
Row 0: 0 + 0; Row 1: 1 + 0, 0 + 1; Row 2: 2 + 0, 0 + 2, 1 + 1; Row 3: 3 + 0, 0 + 3, 2 + 1, 1 + 2; Row 4: 4 + 0, 0 + 4, 3 + 1, 1 + 3, 2 + 2; Row 5: 5 + 0, 0 + 5, 4 + 1, 1 + 4, 3 + 2, 2 + 3; Row 6: 6 + 0, 0 + 6, 5 + 1, 1 + 5, 4 + 2, 2 + 4, 3 + 3; Row 7: 7 + 0, 0 + 7, 6 + 1, 1 + 6, 5 + 2, 2 + 5, 4 + 3, 3 + 4.

8. a. even; b. even; c. odd; d. remains the same; proofs will vary.

9. The 2 possible answers are 48 + 52 and 58 + 42.

## Page 20

10. a. 26; b. 20 + 14; c. 110; strategies will vary.

11. Order of addends in number sentences may vary: Kim—25 + 10 + 7; Harry—25 + 10 + 2 or 25 + 7 + 5.

12. Scores will vary but should not be greater than 200.

## Page 21

13. 4 times

14. Yes. One possible explanation: 2 dozen cookies is 24 cookies. Half of 24 is 12. Linda and her cousins ate 4 + 3 + 6 + 2, or 15 cookies: 15 is greater than 12.

15. 497 – 72. Explanations will vary. One possible explanation: Look at the numbers in the tens place. In the first expression, 3 is less than 4, so regrouping is needed. The answer will have a 2 in the hundreds place. In the second expression, 9 is greater than 7, so no regrouping is needed. The answer will have a 4 in the hundreds place, so the answer to the second expression is greater than the answer to the first expression.

## Page 22

16. News articles will vary.

17. 19 marbles; check students' drawings. There should be 19 marbles hidden in each picture.

18. Check students' drawings; a. Four players were not wearing red socks or red sweatshirts—11 – 7 = 4; b. Four players were not wearing red socks—11 – 7 = 4; c. Eight players were not wearing red sweatshirts—11 – 3 = 8.

## Page 23

19. a. 50; b. 13; c. 50 -13, or 37 more states

20. Grapes cost 45 cents and strawberries cost 55 cents.

21. Chart should resemble one below. Decisions will vary, but may include: Make chocolate

---

chip cookies since the fewest number of students dislike it or make chocolate chip and sugar cookies because those are the two most popular.

| Cookie Type | # Who Like it | # Who Don't Like it |
|---|---|---|
| Chocolate Chip | 23 | 3 |
| Cookies with Raisins | 18 | 8 |
| Sugar Cookies | 20 | 6 |
| Ginger Cookies | 14 | 12 |

## Chapter 3

### Page 27

1. a. 33; b. 49

2. 17; mystery numbers and clues will vary.

3. 131

### Page 28

4. Answers will vary.

5. Answers will vary based on numbers chosen.

6. a. 6; b. 16; c. 36; d. 106; e. 2,586. Pattern: The digit in the ones place doesn't change.

### Page 29

7. 8; 2 + 5 – 3 + 4 = 8

8. Estimates may vary; accept a reasonable range: 1,000–1,200 per hour; 24,000–29,000 per day; 140,000–200,000 per week; 7,000,000–10,000,000 per year.

9. $100; explanations will vary, but may include: Since there are 100 pennies in $1, divide 10,000 by 100. The answer is 100. Check students' drawings.

### Page 30

10. a. $20,000,000 per year; b. about $1,500,000 per month; c. about $50,000 per day

11. about 36,500 days; 10 decades in 100 years; century means "100 years"

12. 5,842,000,000 kilometers

## Chapter 4

### Page 34

1. Examples will vary. Some possible examples: They may use division to determine the number of players to put on each team when playing a game; they may use multiplication

---

to determine the price of 3 pencils when they know the price of 1 pencil.

2. When the rectangle is turned it becomes a 6 by 1 rectangle, described by the multiplication sentence 6 x 1 = 6. The squares can be rearranged to show rectangles representing 2 x 3 = 6 and 3 x 2 =6.

3. 4 x 6 = 24; 8 different rectangles can be made from the 24 squares. The multiplication sentences representing them are: 1 x 24 = 24, 24 x 1 = 24, 2 x 12 = 24, 12 x 2 = 24, 3 x 8 = 24, 8 x 3 = 24, 4 x 6 = 24, 6 x 4 = 24.

### Page 35

4. 120 pictures. Strategies will vary. One possible answer: Think of 24 as 20 + 4, multiply 20 x 5 and 5 x 4 and add the products—100 + 20 = 120.

5. Total Allowance is $40.95. Allowance per week would be as follows:

| Week 1 = 1¢ | Week 5 = 16¢ | Week 9 = $2.56 |
|---|---|---|
| Week 2 = 2¢ | Week 6 = 32¢ | Week 10 = $5.12 |
| Week 3 = 4¢ | Week 7 = 64¢ | Week 11 = $10.24 |
| Week 4 = 8¢ | Week 8 = $1.28 | Week 12 = $20.48 |

6. $36.00; the doubled allowance is $4.95 more than the $3.00-per-week allowance. In Week 14, the doubled allowance would become $81.92, while the $3.00-per-week allowance would remain $3.00; the difference is $78.92. The doubled allowance will grow at a much faster rate.

### Page 36

7. 105 per week; 450 per month; 5,475 per year

8. 375 essays

9. She needs to buy 28 of each fruit and vegetable; a total of 28 x 5, or 140 for the week.

| Food Item | # Needed Each Day | # Needed for Week |
|---|---|---|
| carrots | 4 | 28 |
| potatoes | 4 | 28 |
| apples | 4 | 28 |
| oranges | 4 | 28 |
| bananas | 4 | 28 |
| TOTAL | 20 | 140 |

## Page 37

10. a. One possible strategy: Take off the 2 zeros and multiply—8 x 2 = 16. Add the 2 zeros back to make 1,600. b. 50 x 30 = 1,500; 90 x 70 = 6,300; 60 x 70 = 4,200; c. greater than; students should realize they rounded each factor up, so each estimate is greater than the actual product.

11. Check students' drawings; 24 rooms—4 x 6 = 24; 72 pieces of furniture—24 x 3 = 72

12. Molly needs 3 eggs, 3 slices of cheese, 1½ pieces of ham, 6 tomato slices and 6 pieces of bread.

## Page 38

13. The number 16—4 x 4 = 16; the numbers 4—2 x 2 = 4 and 9—3 x 3 = 9.

14. The square numbers are in a diagonal line from the top left of the chart to the bottom right.

15. Prime numbers between 1 and 25: 2, 3, 5, 7, 11, 13, 17, 19, and 23.

## Page 39

16. 15 ÷ 2 = 7 r1, 16 ÷ 2 = 8, 17 ÷ 2 = 8 r1, 18 ÷ 2 = 9, 19 ÷ 2 = 9 r1, 20 ÷ 2 = 10, 21 ÷ 2 = 10 r1, 22 ÷ 2 = 11, 23 ÷ 2 = 11 r1, 24 ÷ 2 = 12, 25 ÷ 2 = 12 r1, 26 ÷ 2 = 13, 27 ÷ 2 = 13 r1, 28 ÷ 2 = 14, 29 ÷ 2 = 14 r1, 30 ÷ 2 = 15; numbers that can be divided by 2 with no remainder are all even numbers.

17.

| # | Sum of digits | Divisible by 3? | Check |
|---|---|---|---|
| 54 | 5 + 4 = 9 | yes | 54 ÷ 3 = 18 |
| 132 | 1 + 3 + 2 = 6 | yes | 132 ÷ 3 = 44 |
| 516 | 5 + 1 + 6 = 12 | yes | 516 ÷ 3 = 172 |

18. Numbers will vary, but the rule will work each time.

## Page 40

19. 25, 30, 35, 40, 45, 50, 55, 60, 65, 70; the last digit in each number is either 0 or 5; if the last digit of a number is 0 or 5, it is divisible by 5.

20. Examples of numbers divisible by 9 may vary, but may include: 117, 126, 135, 144, 153, 162. The rule should include the idea that if the sum of all the digits is divisible by 9, the number is divisible by 9.

21. Answers will vary; one possible answer: Each of the 5 family members gets 1 whole fish.

The 2 remaining fish are each divided into 5 pieces, with each person receiving ⅕ of both fish. So, each person gets a total of 1⅖ fish.

## Page 41

22. a. 92 ÷ 5 = 18 r2, so 19 adults are needed; b. there are already 3 teachers in the group, so 19 – 3, or 16 parent helpers should be invited; c. the total number of people going is 92 + 3 + 16, or 111. One bus seats 40 people, 2 buses seat 80 people, 3 buses seat 120 people, so 3 buses will be needed.

23. 8-pencil set: about 25¢ each, 12-pencil set: about 22¢ each, 10-pencil set: about 24¢ each. The set with the 12 colored pencils is the best buy.

24. 234 children ÷ 12 freezes/package = 19 r6, so 20 packages would allow each child to get 1 freeze. It will cost 20 x $0.89, or $17.80. The package of 12 costs less than $1.00, so each freeze costs less than $0.10.

## Chapter 5

## Page 45

1. Check students' drawings. The color pattern is yellow-purple-yellow-red; The 10th triangle is purple; the additional 3 triangles are yellow, red, yellow.

2. a. subtract 2; 29, 27, 25; b. add 3; 50, 53, 56; c. 35, 33, 36, 34, 37

3. Student's drawings should show same 2 rows of shapes that appear in Figure 1, page 52.

## Page 46

4. Student's drawings should show a row of shapes identical to each row in Figure 2, page 52.

5. 10 white beads, 5 blue beads, 5 red beads; patterns will vary. One possible pattern: red-white-blue-white.

6. The number of tents increases by 2 each day; they saw 2 tents on Monday; they will see 12 tents on Saturday.

| Day of the Week | Number of Tents |
|---|---|
| M | 2 |
| T | 4 |
| W | 6 |
| TH | 8 |
| F | 10 |

## Page 47

7. Friday: Art; the following week's schedule is:

| Monday | Technology |
|---|---|
| Tuesday | P.E. |
| Wednesday | Library |
| Thursday | Art |
| Friday | Technology |

8. 2004, 2008, 2012, 2016, 2020, 2024

9. Each number in the sequence is the sum of the 2 numbers before it; 55, 89, 144.

## Page 48

10. 165, 1999, 532

11. 160 Payson Rd.; 926-8741; addresses and phone numbers will vary

12. Dates will vary.

## Page 49

13. Draw 4 symbols used to represent a deer. Sentences and pictographs will vary.

14. Hat: 15-8-1; Math is great: 20-8-1-15 16-26  14-25-12-8-1

15. Today is your lucky day!

## Page 50

16. Codes and sentences will vary.

17. Lucky numbers will vary.

18. Patterns and descriptions will vary.

## Chapter 6

## Page 55

1. 2 sections; predictions will vary. A paper folded in half twice will have 4 sections. A paper folded in half 3 times will have 8 sections; Yes, the number of sections would be the same for any size and shape of paper

2. Answers will vary. Sample answer: just as good cut in half—cookies, sandwiches, oranges; ruined if cut in half—clothes, money, books.

3. Check student's drawings; story problems will vary.

## Page 56

4. Number sentences will vary, but may include: ½ + ⅓ + ⅙; ⅓ + ⅙ + ⅙ + ⅑ + ⅑ + ⅑; ½ + ¼ + 1/12 + 1/12 + 1/12.

5. Comparisons will vary.

6. Number sentences for equivalent fractions will vary. Note that students will not be able to find two or more fraction strips equivalent to ⅕, ⅑, 1/12, or 1/16.

## Page 57

7. ⅔, ¾, ⅘, ⅞; ways to check answers will vary, but may include: Compare the fractions using the fraction strips on page 63; Write an equivalent fraction for each using the lowest common denominator (24), and then compare the numerators.

8. Shadow eats ⅓ of a bag of dog food in a week; Rolly will eat 8 bags of food in 8 weeks; Shadow will eat 2⅔ bags of food in 8 weeks.

9. Juan painted ½ the fence, Jaime ⅓, and Joel ⅙.

## Page 58

10. 3 people; 1 can tomato sauce, ½ can tomato paste, 2 cups chopped tomatoes, 1 pound spaghetti

11. ¾ of a cupcake; drawings will vary.

12. Pictures will vary. One possible picture:

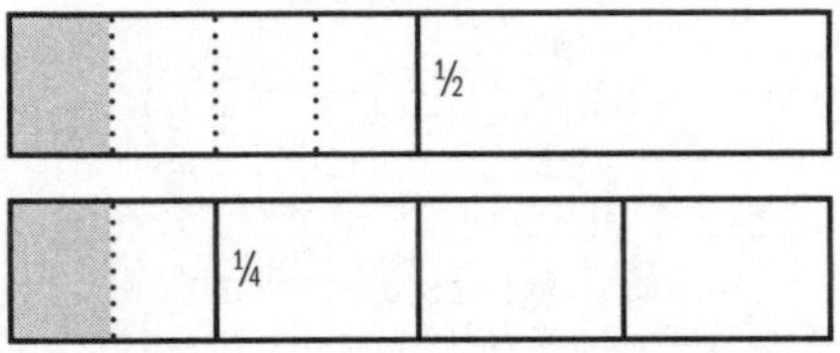

| | | | | ½ |

| | ¼ | | | |

## Page 59

13. Devon will eat ⅔ of the pizza, and Troy will eat ⅓.

14. Designs will vary but may include the following ratios: 2 to 8, 4 to 16, 8 to 32, and so on

15. Answers will vary, but may include: at the deli counter in a grocery store—0.25 pounds, 1.5 pounds, 2.75 pounds; at athletic events—a time of 14.12 minutes, a length of 7 ft 8.25 in., a batting average of 0.345.

## Page 60

16. 97,542.1; 1.24579

17. The same amount of each square is colored; check students' drawings: 0.40, 0.33, 0.75.

18. 80%; questions will vary.

## Page 61

19. Check student's drawings.

20. potato, apple, watermelon

21. 10.1 miles; $25.25

## Chapter 7

## Page 66

1. Items and estimates will vary, but may include: the face of a watch [same size as quarter], the bottom of a pencil or marker [smaller], and the bottom of a paper cup [larger].

2. Comparisons will vary. Students should indicate whether the drawn objects were larger, smaller, or the same size as the actual items.

3. Lists will vary. Descriptions of rectangles will vary but should include two of the following: 4 sides, 2 pairs of parallel sides, 4 right angles [or square corners].

## Page 67

4. a. #1 or #3; b. #3; c. #4

5. Descriptions will vary. Sample response for square: each of 4 corners is a square corner, or a right angle; all 4 sides are the same length.

6. Drawings should show: a. a scalene triangle, b. an isosceles triangle, c. an equilateral triangle.

## Page 68

7. Predictions will vary. The top shape is a triangle, the middle shape is a rhombus, and the bottom shape is a rectangle.

8. Predictions and sentences will vary.

9. Answers will vary.

## Page 69

10. Answers and drawings will vary. A possible solution is:

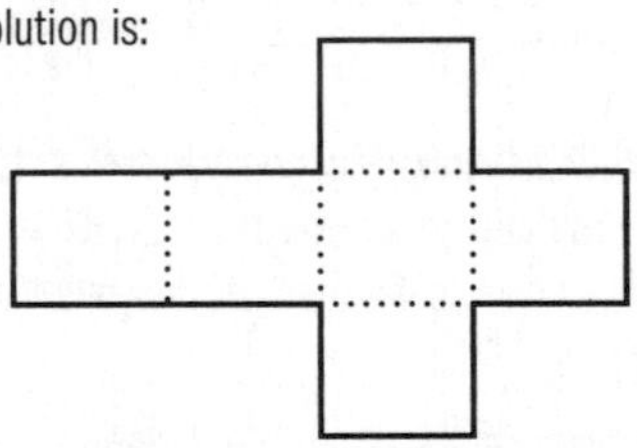

11. Answers may vary. Possible answers include: measure the angle of the empty space of the pie and find the piece that has that angle; trace the outline of the empty space of the pie and match its outline to one of the pieces; piece B is the missing piece.

12. Polygons drawn will vary; the number of sides in each polygon is equal to the number of angles.

## Page 70

13. penta—5; hexa—6, hepta—7; octa—8; nona—9; deca—10; the pentagon is the 5-sided shape, the hexagon the 6-sided shape, and so on.

14. Examples will vary but may include: triangles—yield signs, rectangles—doors and windows, pentagons—school crossing signs, heptagons—arrows.

15. Memory clues will vary but polygons include: pentagon, hexagon, heptagon, octagon, nonagon, and decagon.

## Page 71

16. Check student's drawings; number of concentric shapes drawn will vary.

17. Drawings will vary but should not overlap or contain gaps.

18. Drawings will vary.

## Page 72

19. Answers will vary; make sure pictures match the number of triangles used.

20. See tangram puzzle on page 78 for how the pieces should fit.

21. a. 3 different shapes—triangles, a square, and a rhombus; b. 3 different sizes of triangles; c. 2 small triangles and the square form a triangle congruent to a large triangle.

## Page 73

22.

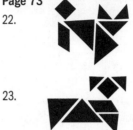

23.

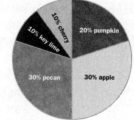

24. Student's should have a paper cup if they follow the directions. NOTE: Students may need to see the steps modeled or have them verbalized.

## Chapter 8

## Page 80

1. Bar graphs will vary; check their accuracy.

2. Line graphs will vary; check their accuracy.

3.

20% pumpkin; 10% cherry; 10% key lime; 30% pecan; 30% apple

## Page 81

4. Horizontal Axis: PLAYING SOCCER; Vertical Axis: DRAWING; Ralph likes to draw more than he likes playing soccer and more than Anya likes drawing; Anya likes to play soccer more than she likes drawing and more than Ralph likes playing soccer.

5.

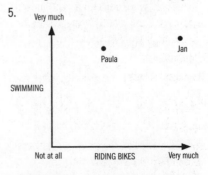

6. Survey questions and graphs will vary.

**Page 82**

7. a rhombus or diamond

8. Designs and coordinates will vary.

9. Charts will vary.

**Page 83**

10. Charts will vary.

11. Steps will vary, but may include: 1. Write down the birthday of everyone in the class. 2. List the months and make a tally mark next to the month for each birthday. 3. Count the tally marks to find which month has the greatest number. One possible response: A chart would be helpful for listing the months and making a tally.

12.

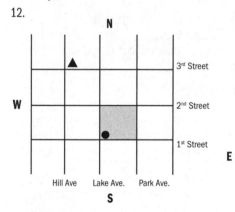

**Page 84**

13. Maps and directions will vary.

14. Legends will vary but should include: triangle = school, square = park, and circle = pond. Bonus: Check students' maps.

15. 8 miles; maps will vary, but the distances between the towns should be the same on every map: Riverville to Lakeville—5 cm; Lakeville to Redville—7 cm; Blueville to Riverville or Redville—about 4.5 cm.

**Page 85**

16. Answers may vary, but may include: Poptown is about as far from Strawtown as Strawtown is from Globetown; Sandtown is about as far from Poptown as Looptown is from Globetown. Looptown is about as far from Rocktown as Rocktown is from Sandtown.

17. Maps will vary.

18. Designs will vary.

**Chapter 9**

**Page 91**

1. sun: hours and days, moon: days and months, seasons: months and years

2. Less than 365; that's about how long it takes Earth to complete 1 orbit around the sun; the time it takes Earth to orbit the sun is closer to 365 1/4 days than 365 days, so every 4 years (leap year) a day is added to adjust the calendar.

3. Answers will vary, but may include: There are 12 months in a year; days are measured by a multiple of 12 [24 hours in a day]; seconds and minutes are measured in a multiple of 12 [60 seconds in a minute, 60 minutes in an hour]; other numbers used to measure time may include: 7—days in a week; 4—weeks in a month and quarters in an hour.

**Page 92**

4. Answers will vary.

5. a. Mondays: 8th, 15th, 22nd, 29th; b. the first Saturday will be the 7th.

6. A year on Mars is nearly twice as long as a year on Earth; number of days old and age in Mars years will vary depending on age, but age in Mars years will be roughly half of age in Earth years. For example, a child who is 10 years old is about 3,650 days old. That's a little more than 5 years in Mars years.

**Page 93**

7. 9 hours of sleep; bedtime 9:00 P.M.; 6:00 A.M.; Bonus: twice

8. Wake up: 0700, School: 0800, Lunch: 1200, Basketball: 1500, Dinner: 1700, Homework: 1900, Bedtime: 2200; Bonus: Schedules will vary.

9. Answers will vary, but may include: telephone, television, microcomputer, radio, microwave, automobile, train, and airplane.

**Page 94**

10. Greg: 12:04 A.M.; Peg: 12/31/1999; Greg: 1/1/2000

11. About 15 minutes

12.

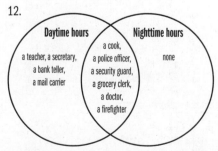

**Page 95**

13. Answers will vary according to starting time, one possible schedule: Game 1—8:30, Game 2—10:15, Game 3—12:00, Game 4—1:45, Game 5—3:30.

14. Schedules will vary; one possible schedule:

| Time | Activity |
| --- | --- |
| after school until 6:00 | play outside |
| 6:00–6:30 | eat dinner |
| 6:30–7:00 | study |
| 7:00–8:00 | do chores, talk on phone, get ready for bed |
| 8:00–8:30 | read |
| 8:30 | go to bed |

15. 15 peanuts = 1 nickel; 30 peanuts = 1 dime; 75 peanuts = 1 quarter; 300 peanuts = 1 dollar; the value of 100 peanuts would be less than 40¢.

**Page 96**

16. Answers will vary. Students may set up a system in which value is related to size—the smaller the object, the lesser the value, and it may take several small objects to equal the value of a large object.

17. penny [Lincoln], quarter [Washington], nickel [Jefferson], dime [Roosevelt]; the value of the 4 coins is 41 cents.

18. a. quarter/dime card and nickel card; b. 10 pennies card and nickel card; c. 2 nickels card and 2 pennies card; d. quarter/dime card and dime/nickel card; e. dime/nickel card and 3 pennies card

**Page 97**

19. Answers will vary.

20. Answers will vary. One possible response: Raul and Ariel need to think about whether they want to spend any money on food or games, and whether they have enough time to make the unlimited number of rides worthwhile. In considering time, they should think about the number of rides they want to go on, how long they would have to wait in line for each ride, and how long each ride may take.

21. 1 CD: 11 days; 2 CDs: 21 days

**Page 98**

22. Answers will vary, but total cost in either answer shouldn't exceed $50; a: $9.95 more for skates; b: $79.98 more for dollhouse kit

**23.**

| Item | Sale Price | Regular Price |
|---|---|---|
| 2 CD's | $21.00 | $25.98 |
| Running Shoes | $25.75 | $51.50 |
| In-Line Skates | $59.95 | $119.90 |
| Helmet | $19.95 | $39.90 |
| Dollhouse and 4 dolls | $129.98 | $129.98 |
| 3 books | $12.00 | $14.55 |

(Delia's Dollhouses shouldn't be advertising sale prices.)

24. a. 85¢; b. $1.01; c. no change; d. $1.25

## Chapter 10

### Page 103

1. Answers will vary. Solutions will likely involve the creation or use of a standard unit of measurement.

2. Answers will vary.

3. Answers will vary; some possible answers: building houses, making clothing, giving medicine, planning a space shuttle flight; explanations will vary.

### Page 104

4. Answers will vary.

5. Answers will vary.

6. Estimates will vary; 16 pennies = 1 foot.

### Page 105

7. 36 inches; answers will vary.

8. Answers will vary, but may include: inches—pencils, jeans [waist and inseam measurements]; feet—people's heights, rooms; yards—football fields, distances on playground.

9. Estimates will vary; you can multiply the measure of your own outstretched arms by 10; estimates will vary; explanations will vary, but students should recognize that an estimate based on a known measure will more likely be closer to the actual measure than one that is not based on a known measure.

### Page 106

10. Answers will vary.

11. Estimates will vary. It is most likely that the sum of finger and thumb lengths will be greater than the length of the foot.

12. calculator

### Page 107

13. Answers will vary.

14. Perimeters will vary; the perimeter may or may not change; the greatest perimeter of a figure they can make is 18 inches—a 1 x 8 rectangle; the least perimeter of a figure they can make is 12 inches—a 2 x 4 rectangle.

15. Figures will vary; however, the area of each figure will be 25 square inches.

### Page 108

16. Answers will vary.

17.

| Figure | Area (sq. cm) | Perimeter (cm) |
|---|---|---|
| A | 12 | 16 |
| B | 12 | 14 |
| C | 16 | 16 |
| D | 12 | 16 |
| E | 12 | 26 |
| F | 12 | 18 |

18. Answers will vary.

### Page 109

19. 1 tablespoon = ½ ounce, 1 cup = 8 ounces, 1 pint = 16 ounces, 1 quart = 32 ounces, 1 gallon = 128 ounces

20. cool; warm; warm; hot; cold

21. 31 degrees

### Page 110

22. Cereal is measured by weight [ounces]. Two boxes the same size may not contain the same amount, but they will weigh the same.

23. Check students' drawings. Students should recognize that the same-size jar will hold a greater number of small objects than large objects.

24. Answers may vary. One possible answer: Find something that weighs 1 pound, such as a 1-pound package of butter, and compare the weight of that object to the weight of the apples.

## Chapter 11

### Page 116

1.

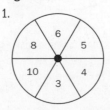

2.

| 6 | 1 | 8 |
|---|---|---|
| 7 | 5 | 3 |
| 2 | 9 | 4 |

3. Magic squares will vary; methods may vary but may include: guess and check, writing down all the combinations of 3 numbers less than 10 that have a sum of 15 and using that list to place the numbers in the square.

### Page 117

4. 2 x 2 x 2 = 8 different lunches

5. The boy is the one with red hair, and the girl is the one with black hair. Possible explanation: if 1 of them is not telling the truth, and says the opposite of what she or he means, then the other one must also not be telling the truth, since there is 1 boy and 1 girl.

6. Even; even; odd. Possible rule: If birth year and calendar year are both odd or both even, the age will be an even number. If one of the years is odd and one even, the age will be an odd number.

### Page 118

7. Answers will vary but may include: 29 in. of rain, 10 in. of snow; 28 in. of rain, 20 in. of snow; 27 in. of rain, 30 in. of snow; 26 in. of rain, 40 in. of snow; 25 in. of rain, 50 in. of snow.

8. 5 trips

9. a. 7 x 8 = 56, 8 x 7 = 56, 56 ÷ 7 = 8, 56 ÷ 8 = 7, b. 6 x 9 = 54, 9 x 6 = 54, 54 ÷ 6 = 9, 54 ÷ 9 = 6, c. 8 + 9 = 17, 9 + 8 = 17, 17 − 9 = 8, 17 − 8 = 9

### Page 119

10. Values of names will vary; value for *math is great* = 3¼ + ¼ + 5 + 2 + 2¼ + 4¾ + 1¾ + 4½ + 1¼ + ¼ + 5 = 30¼.

11. 3 socks: the first sock would be either white or black; the second sock might match the first sock, or it might not; the third sock will either match the first sock, the second sock, both socks, or neither sock, but in that case, the first 2 socks would have to match.

12. Bruce was right. There are 4 cards greater than 20 in the deck of cards, so Magda has 4 chances out of 24 cards, or a 1:6 chance of pulling a number greater than 20. There are 12 cards with even numbers, so Bruce has 12 chances out of 24 cards to pull an even number from the deck, or a 1:2 chance.